1914–15

German Infantryman
VERSUS
Russian Infantryman

COMBAT

Robert Forczyk

First published in Great Britain in 2015 by Osprey Publishing,
PO Box 883, Oxford, OX1 9PL, UK
PO Box 3985, New York, NY 10185-3985, USA
E-mail: info@ospreypublishing.com

Osprey Publishing is part of the Osprey Group

A CIP catalogue record for this book is available from the British Library

Print ISBN: 978 1 4728 0654 3
PDF ebook ISBN: 978 1 4728 0655 0
ePub ebook ISBN: 978 1 4728 0656 7

Index by Mark Swift
Typeset in Univers, Sabon and Adobe Garamond Pro
Maps by bounford.com
Originated by PDQ Media, Bungay, UK
Printed in China through Shanghai Offset Printing Ltd

15 16 17 18 19   10 9 8 7 6 5 4 3 2 1

Osprey Publishing is supporting the Woodland Trust, the UK's leading woodland conservation charity, by funding the dedication of trees.

www.ospreypublishing.com

Author's note

Dedicated to MAJ Michael L. Donahue, HHB, XVIII ABN Corps, KIA 16 September 2014, Kabul, Afghanistan.

Editor's note

All dates quoted follow the Gregorian calendar (rather than the Julian calendar still used in Tsarist Russia) and all measurements in this book are in metric. For ease of comparison please refer to the following conversion table:

1km = 0.62 miles
1m = 1.09yd / 3.28ft
1cm = 0.39in
1mm = 0.04in
1kg = 2.20lb / 35.27oz

Artist's note

Readers may care to note that the original paintings from which the artwork plates in this book were prepared are available for private sale. All reproduction copyright whatsoever is retained by the Publishers. All enquiries should be addressed to:

Scorpio, 158 Mill Road, Hailsham, East Sussex BN27 2SH, UK
Email: scorpiopaintings@btinternet.com

The Publishers regret that they can enter into no correspondence upon this matter.

Comparative ranks

German	Russian	Translation
Generalfeldmarschall	general-fel'dmarshal	field marshal
Generaloberst	n/a	colonel-general
General der Infanterie/Artillerie/Kavallerie	general ot infanterii/artillerii/kavalerii	general of infantry/artillery
Generalleutnant	general-leytenant	lieutenant general
Generalmajor	general-mayor	major general
Oberst	polkovnik	colonel
Oberstleutnant	podpolkovnik	lieutenant colonel
Major	maijor	major
Hauptmann	kapitan	captain
n/a	shtabs-kapitan	staff captain
Oberleutnant	poruchik	first lieutenant
Leutnant	podporuchik	second lieutenant
Fähnrich	praporshchik (wartime only)	ensign (commissioned)
n/a	podpraporshchik	ensign
Feldwebel	fel'dfebel'	first sergeant
Vizefeldwebel	starshi unterofitser	senior sergeant
Sergeant	n/a	sergeant
Unteroffizier	mladshi unterofitser	junior sergeant
Gefreiter	yefreitor	corporal
Musketier/Grenadier	ryadovoy	private
Wehrmann	n/a	recruit

CONTENTS

Introduction

German infantry in the attack, East Prussia, August 1914. Note that these German troops are more dispersed since they are under artillery fire – which does not appear to be all that effective. (Scherl / SZ Photo)

This study examines the contest between German and Russian infantrymen in the opening six months of World War I on the Eastern Front primarily through the lens of the Russian 27th Infantry Division (*27-ya Pekhotnaya Diviziya*) and their German opponents in three early actions. Although the German superiority at the operational level of warfare has been discussed in a number of works, the tactical dynamics of the Eastern Front in World War I have generally received little attention in English-language historiography. Both armies were overwhelmingly composed of infantrymen, although the artillery provided essential fire support. Other branches, such as the engineers,

One day after the German declaration of war on Russia, Generaloberst Maximilian von Prittwitz (1848–1917) took command of 8. Armee, at its headquarters at Bartenstein (now Bartoszyce), 50km south of Königsberg (now Kaliningrad). Primarily an administrator and staff officer who was ill-suited for either independent command or leading outnumbered forces in toe-to-toe combat against a superior foe, the 65-year-old Prittwitz's only combat experience was as a junior officer against the Austrians in 1866 and the French in 1870–71, but he was a successful courtier who managed to secure an army command. (TopFoto)

played a lesser role; cavalry was in tactical decline due to the advent of the machine gun; and aviation was still too primitive in 1914 to influence ground combat. Tactically, at regimental level and below, there was little to distinguish between the two sides' infantry. The opposing foot-soldiers were armed with rifles and machine guns that were roughly comparable in terms of quality, and their tactical organizations were also quite similar. Leadership and training were important factors, but the notion that German infantry were always superior to their Russian opponents in these areas has become an entrenched over-simplification. While operational manoeuvring would set the stage for the campaign in East Prussia in 1914, the outcome would be determined at the tactical level by the clash of German and Russian infantrymen.

In response to the Austro-Hungarian mobilization against Serbia, due to the crisis brought on by the assassination of the Archduke Franz Ferdinand, Russia initiated General Mobilization on 31 July 1914. The next day, 1 August, Imperial Germany declared war on Russia. Since the German leadership decided to make their main effort in the West against France, the

Russian infantry in training, advancing with bayonets charged. Russian tactical doctrine still enjoyed a preference for shock action with cold steel, which the Germans had moved away from in favour of 'fire tactics'. (Author)

Großer Generalstab (General Staff) deployed only a single army – Generaloberst Maximilian von Prittwitz's 8. Armee, possessing 218,000 troops once fully mobilized – to defend East Prussia. When Prittwitz took command on 2 August, 8. Armee consisted of three corps of the Stehendes Heer (Standing Army): I., XVII. and XX. Armeekorps. After mobilization began, it was reinforced with I. Reservekorps, the Landwehrkorps, one independent Reserve division and one cavalry division. Thus, Prittwitz had a total of 57 infantry regiments to defend East Prussia, of which 25 were Stehendes Heer, 12 Reserve and 20 Landwehr (Territorial Army). There were also four *Jäger-Bataillone*, one per corps.

Consequently, the German military leadership adopted a 'win–hold–win' strategy for the Eastern Front, with the mission of 8. Armee simply to hold off the more numerous Russian armies until the campaign in the West was decided and reinforcements could arrive to mount a counter-offensive. This would be no small undertaking and the Germans were rightly concerned that Russian mass – the infamous 'steamroller' – might overwhelm 8. Armee if given time. Yet the German leadership knew that Russia would commit two-thirds of its forces against the Austro-Hungarian Army in Galicia and that it would take Russia about 60 days after the beginning of General Mobilization to mobilize some 70 infantry divisions. Under these conditions, the Großer Generalstab assessed that it was unlikely that the Russian Army could mount a serious offensive into East Prussia in the first month after the outbreak of war, but that 8. Armee would be hard-pressed by the second month of the

General ot kavalerii Yakov G. Zhilinski (1853–1918) would be unable effectively to co-ordinate or sustain the operations of First and Second armies. Instead, 8. Armee would be allowed to fight one Russian army at a time; much the same would occur at army level, where individual Russian corps were poorly co-ordinated. Lack of effective command and control would reduce the Russian steamroller to a series of piecemeal efforts from the beginning. (TopFoto)

war. Thus by design, the German effort on the Eastern Front for the first few months of World War I was a calculated risk, with German forces heavily outnumbered by their Russian opponents and forced to play for time.

Yet the German Großer Generalstab was unaware that General ot kavalerii Yakov G. Zhilinski, Chief of the Russian General Staff (*Glavny Shtab*), had assured the French Général Joseph Joffre in joint discussions prior to the war that the Russian Army would mount an offensive into East Prussia within 15 days after General Mobilization was declared. It was a foolhardy promise but once war was declared, the Russians felt honour-bound to act upon it. While a hasty offensive would exact a cost in terms of logistical sustainment for the campaign's opening phase, the Russians had sufficient active-duty forces in the region that they felt they could mount a 'come-as-you-are' operation and trust to superior numbers to carry the day. This Russian decision to mount a quick thrust into East Prussia from both Lithuania and Poland placed

A young soldier of Reserve-Infanterie-Regiment Nr. 12, a Brandenburg formation that initially fought in the West before being transferred to the East in December 1914. (S. J. Perry Collection)

8. Armee in greater peril earlier than the Großer Generalstab had anticipated. On the other hand, the Russian General Staff decided to place the main offensive emphasis against the Austro-Hungarians in Galicia and halved the forces to be employed against East Prussia from four down to just two armies.

Russia's First Army, stationed in Lithuania and commanded by General ot kavalerii Pavel K. von Rennenkampf (1854–1918), was best positioned to mount a rapid assault into East Prussia on short notice. Initially, First Army consisted of just three active corps (3rd, 4th and 20th), along with a separate infantry division and five cavalry divisions, but on 22 August 2nd Corps was transferred from Second Army to Rennenkampf's First Army. Altogether, First Army started the invasion of East Prussia with 40 infantry regiments, making it slightly smaller than 8. Armee. However, the *Glavny Shtab* also committed Second Army, based in Poland and commanded by General ot kavalerii Aleksandr V. Samsonov (1859–1914), to invade East Prussia from the south. On paper, Rennenkampf and Samsonov could commit a total of 76 first-line infantry regiments against just 40 German infantry regiments, more than half of which were Reserve or Landwehr. The General Staff's concept was to conduct a simultaneous pincer attack from the south and east into East Prussia, crushing 8. Armee in between the jaws of the two Russian

armies. Zhilinski, who as Chief of the General Staff had pledged to the French that the Russian Army would invade East Prussia by the 15th day of General Mobilization, was placed in command of the newly created North-Western Front that was now directed to make good on this promise. Yet the concept was marred by two intrinsic problems. First, the heavily forested Masurian Lakes district, some 75km from north to south, lay in between Rennenkampf's First Army and Samsonov's Second Army, preventing close co-operation. Second, Samsonov's Second Army was larger than Rennenkampf's, with five corps, but it would require additional time to prepare before it could begin its offensive. However, the Russian offensive into East Prussia would be unsynchronized from the start due to terrain and logistical factors which would make it impossible to translate the overall Russian numerical superiority into a decisive factor on the battlefield.

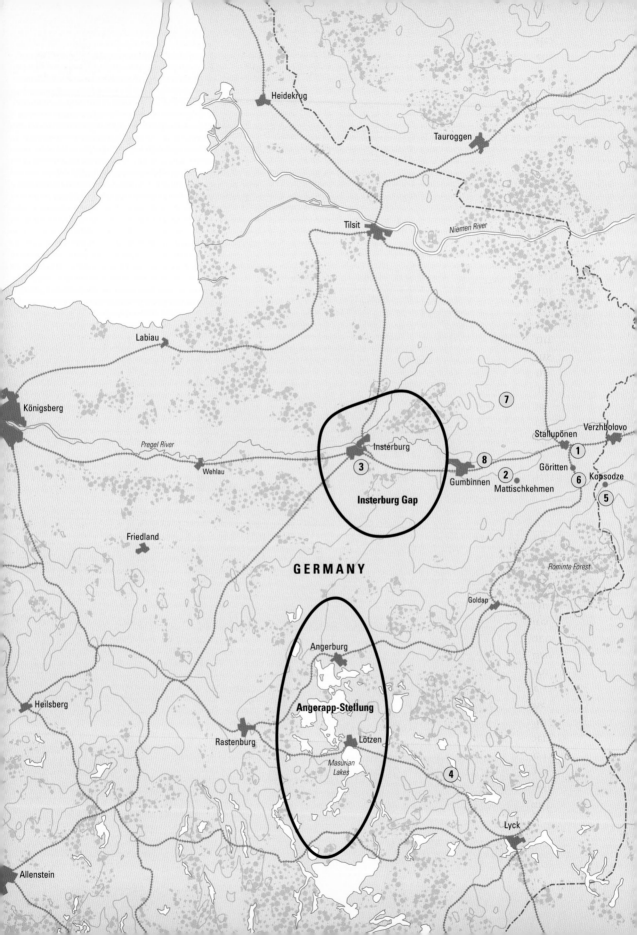

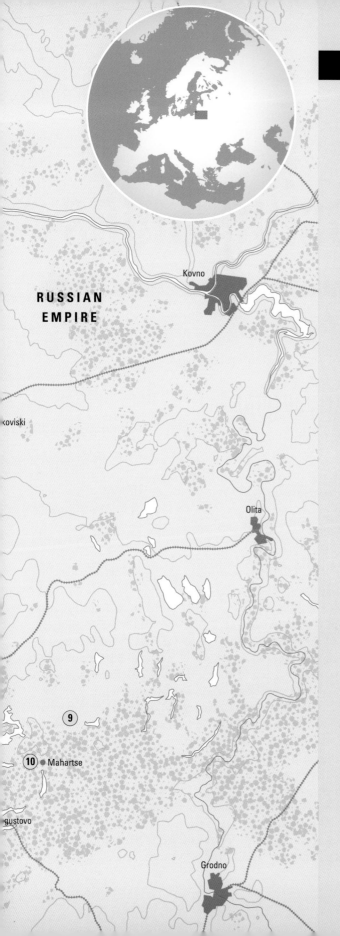

RUSSIAN
EMPIRE

Kovno

koviski

Olita

9

10 Mahartse

gustovo

Grodno

Northern Sector, Eastern Front, 1914–15

1   17 August 1914: The battle of Stallupönen (now Nesterov, Russia). 3rd Corps crosses the East Prussian border, but is quickly ambushed in a counter-attack by I. Armeekorps. 2. Infanterie-Division hits the flank of 27th Infantry Division and badly mauls the 105th Infantry Regiment *Orenburg*.

2   20 August 1914: The battle of Gumbinnen (now Gusev, Russia). 8. Armee launches a full-scale counter-offensive. 2. Infanterie-Division mounts another flanking manoeuvre that catches 28th Infantry Division unprepared and routs it with heavy casualties. However, the attack by XVII. Armeekorps against the centre of the Russian line held by 27th Infantry Division at Mattischkehmen (now Sovkhoznoye, Russia) is repulsed.

3   25 August 1914: 3rd Corps captures Insterburg (now Chernyakhovsk, Russia).

4   7–10 September 1914: The first battle of the Masurian Lakes. 8. Armee conducts a counter-offensive against First Army's left flank between Lyck (now Ełk, Poland) and Lötzen (now Giżycko, Poland). I. Armeekorps defeats the newly arrived 3rd Siberian Corps and 22nd Corps and threatens to envelop First Army's left flank; Rennenkampf orders a general retreat.

5   31 October 1914: The battle of Kopsodze (now Kaupiškiai, Lithuania). 27th Infantry Division mounts a night attack against a regiment from I. Reservekorps, which has advanced across the border into Lithuania. However, the Germans are alert and repel the attack.

6   7 November 1914: When the Germans decide to pull back across the border into East Prussia, 3rd Corps pursues. 27th Infantry Division captures the village of Göritten (now Pushkino, Russia) but is almost immediately counter-attacked by a much superior force comprising the bulk of I. Reservekorps. After fighting off the Germans for eight hours with negligible support, the Russian division retreats.

7   7–9 February 1915: The second battle of the Masurian Lakes. 9. Armee mounts a major winter counter-offensive against Tenth Army's right flank north of Gumbinnen and shatters 3rd Corps.

8   10 February 1915: 20th Corps belatedly begins its retreat towards Augustovo (now Augustów, Poland).

9   15 February 1915: XXI. Armeekorps manages to outflank the retreating 20th Corps and blocks its movement through the Augustovo Forest.

10   16 February 1915: 20th Corps mounts a desperate break-out effort, using the badly depleted 27th Infantry Division to assault the German blocking position at Mahartse (now Podmacharce, Poland). Part of an over-extended German regiment is defeated and the village taken, but the Russians lack the strength to break completely through the ring closing around 20th Corps. Only a few thousand survivors escape, but the rest of the corps is isolated and eventually forced to surrender.

The Opposing Sides

OPERATIONAL DOCTRINE

Russian

Russian pre-war operational-level doctrine was not very aggressive and reflected an 'advance, dig in and evaluate' approach to warfare. Neither Russian commanders nor logistics were up for fast-moving manoeuvre warfare. Despite the Russians' overall 2–1 numerical superiority in infantry, 8. Armee would enjoy a significant edge due to its ability to shift forces around by rail using 'interior lines', while the Russian armies advancing into East Prussia were limited to a walking pace.

The Russians could only commit nine infantry corps, or 33 per cent of their combat forces, against 8. Armee in East Prussia at the outset of the war. Fully 52 per cent of the Russian mobile forces were directed against the Austro-Hungarians in Galicia and another 15 per cent had to be set aside to watch the Turkish and Romanian borders. The 60-year-old Rennenkampf, of Baltic-German lineage, had considerable recent combat experience as a divisional and corps-level commander during the 1904–05 Russo-Japanese War and was a decent, if not great, choice to lead an army-sized force. Zhilinski did not trust the seven newly raised reserve infantry divisions that were assigned to First Army and ordered that they remain in Lithuania; these divisions would not be fully formed until M+30 and they were ordered to conduct additional training before use in combat. In addition, each regular infantry regiment was ordered to detach one or two companies to protect the lines of communication, which amounted to over 5,000 infantrymen. This left Rennenkampf with seven first-line infantry divisions with a total of 114 infantry battalions to mount the invasion of East Prussia, against 8. Armee's 144 infantry battalions.

While the addition of Samsonov's Second Army theoretically gave Zhilinski's North-Western Front a numerical advantage against 8. Armee,

Russian strategic command and control in August 1914 was so laughable that the operations of these invasion forces were merely concurrent, not co-ordinated. The whole notion of the Russian 'Steam Roller' was more an invention of German propaganda than reality in East Prussia in August 1914. In fact, the German infantry would often enjoy numerical parity or even superiority in the opening battles in the East.

Russian infantry pause during the early stages of the invasion of East Prussia, August 1914. Note the soldier with the furled regimental colours. (Scherl / SZ Photo)

German

Unlike the German armies on the Western Front, 8. Armee had no prepared war plan to execute and Prittwitz was authorized to act at his discretion. The Großer Generalstab knew that the Russians had superior forces stationed opposite East Prussia, in Lithuania and Poland, but German intelligence estimates believed that the Russian Army was not capable of rapid movement in the early days of hostilities and that their level of training and efficiency were much inferior to those of the German Army. Indeed, German pre-war intelligence estimates about the Russian Army displayed assessments based more on anti-Slavic racial bias than hard facts. The official German intelligence estimate for Russia in 1913 described Russian officers as 'physically and mentally lazy' and asserted that Russian soldiers were 'mentally slow and lacked initiative' (quoted in Zuber 2011: 136–37). In short, the German Army had a low opinion of the Russian Army's capabilities, based upon racial stereotypes. Thus, the German strategic risk on the Eastern Front was based on assumptions that the opposing Russian combat units were of inferior quality compared to German combat units and that Russian superior numbers would be slow to move into action.

Key elements of German operational-level doctrine included a willingness to use Reserve and Landwehr infantry in battle from the beginning and a

A German unit advances along a rail line in the early stages of World War I. In East Prussia 8. Armee was able to enhance its operational-level manoeuvrability by using internal railway lines to shuffle troops to fight off the Russian First and Second armies. By relying on rail movement, German infantry were often less fatigued than their Russian opponents. (Nik Cornish at www.stavka.org.uk)

reliance upon railroads to shuffle corps-size formations around rapidly. German strategy in the East did allow for fortifications such as the Angerapp-Stellung to channelize and impede an enemy advance across the border into East Prussia, but these were only intended to buy time for 8. Armee's mobile reserves to arrive and launch vicious counter-attacks against an enemy's exposed flanks. Unlike the Western campaign, the German forces in East Prussia would be fighting on friendly soil, which offered advantages in terms of intelligence and logistics. It was believed that recurrent counter-attacks could keep a superior foe off balance long enough and prevent the loss of key terrain. Oddly, the Germans developed no real doctrine for a mobile delay, and did not create special border units that could act as a covering force at the outset of a war – a major omission for 8. Armee. Furthermore, the German Army deployed only a single cavalry division in East Prussia, even though cavalry was well suited for mobile delay operations. In fact, German doctrine was rather immature for the kind of mission assigned to 8. Armee.

RECRUITMENT AND MOTIVATION

Russian

Imperial Russia introduced universal military conscription in 1874 – although a number of ethnic groups and special categories were exempt from service – with terms of service in the infantry reduced from five to three years in 1906. Males became eligible for service aged 21 and if selected, served three years on active duty, followed by 15 in the reserves. In 1914 roughly 86 per cent of Russia's troops were of Russian, Belarusian or Ukrainian origin; Muslims from Central Asia and the Caucasus were usually excluded – but there were exceptions – while Jews were conscripted, but usually treated poorly, and virtually none became officers. In peacetime, no unit was allowed to have more than 30 per cent minorities. Until 1910, Russian Army units conscripted able-bodied males across Western Russia and Siberia and sent them to units away from their home areas, but in that year a new territorial system was instituted and the Warsaw and Vilna military districts were established. The regular divisions that would comprise Rennenkampf's First Army – such as 27th Infantry Division, home of the three Russian regiments featured in this book – were recruited outside the Vilna Military District, but many reservists were conscripted inside the region. Yet since the Tsarist government regarded the Poles and Lithuanians as potentially unreliable, the General Staff was hesitant to use reserve divisions near the front line. The pool of available manpower greatly exceeded the needs of the Russian Army, which conscripted only about 35 per cent of potential recruits each year. Like the German Army, some individuals volunteered for active service, in exchange for a two-year obligation and choice of unit. However, unlike in Germany, conscription in Russia was generally regarded as a curse, not a patriotic duty. Enlisted conscripts were held in low esteem by many civilians and the use of troops against protestors and striking workers during the 1905 Revolution had done nothing to burnish this image.

Although many Russian infantrymen in 1914–15 were illiterate, there were some urban-born conscripts with the aptitude for writing letters home. The Russian Army of 1914 had failed to consider how it might use newspapers and other information media to inform the troops and raise fighting spirit and consequently, the Russian infantryman had little interest in the outcome. Given the shock of violent urban unrest during the 1905 Revolution, the Russian Army preferred peasant conscripts, rather than males from the cities, who were more likely to be affected by revolutionary agitation; in 1914, 62 per cent of soldiers came from peasant backgrounds, but only 4 per cent from factory workers. However, reliance on soldiers who could not read pro-revolutionary pamphlets meant that about 40 per cent of Russian infantrymen in 1914 were illiterate. Furthermore, those troops with some education were usually assigned to the artillery, cavalry or signals troops, leaving the infantry with the mass of illiterates. When mobilization began, the Army was flooded with even more peasant conscripts, raising the illiteracy level to 61 per cent overall; in contrast, only 0.04 per cent of German conscripts were illiterate – this was a dangerous discrepancy. (Author)

Once conscripted, the Russian infantry recruit underwent four months of individual training at a regimental depot; this training included drill, physical training and initial weapons familiarization. Once individual training was completed, recruits passed through 6–8 weeks of company-level training, followed by four weeks of battalion-level and two weeks of regimental-level training. After this, any conscripts that had displayed above-average aptitude might be assigned to the infantry regiment's machine-gun detachment or one of the small number of specialized support billets. The rest of the conscripts would serve out the rest of their time in service as riflemen. Overall, Russian infantry training turned out excellent 'field soldiers' who were well adapted to the rigours of campaigning. Although the lack of widespread literacy limited what the Russian conscripts could be trained in, their ability to march on little or no rations and in the worst weather conditions gave them a certain advantage over their German infantry opponents.

The Russian Army had made considerable efforts to create its own military traditions in order to enhance *esprit de corps* and this had achieved some success in the pre-war regular units. Even so, Russian training and morale were undermined by a number of factors. First, the Army did not invest sufficiently in constructing proper barracks for the troops, who were often housed either in dilapidated structures or civilian housing. In order to save money, many units skimped on simple requirements such as blankets and firewood. Second, the Russian government tried to reduce overall military

A Russian infantry regiment receiving its colours. Note the Orthodox chaplains observing the ceremony – each regiment had several to minister to the troops and promote love of country, church and Tsar. (Courtesy of the Central Museum of the Armed Forces, Moscow via Stavka)

A pre-war postcard of Danziger Infanterie-Regiment Nr. 128. The Germans were adept at making military life seem appealing, which helped to mould recruits into soldiers. In contrast, service in the Russian Army was considered extremely undesirable by many peasant youths. In 1914 most German soldiers in 8. Armee were literate, even if they came from farming communities in East Prussia. Due to carefully cultivated traditions of militarism in Imperial Germany, service in the Army was held in high regard and the level of patriotism and sense of duty – particularly at the beginning of World War I – was remarkably high even among conscripts. Prussians were also noted for a well-honed sense of discipline and conscripts from rural communities had not been exposed to the kind of socialist agitation that was more evident from recruits from industrial areas such as the Ruhr. Furthermore, the troops of 8. Armee were the only German troops being asked to defend their own native soil at the outset of World War I, which gave them a personal stake in the outcome of the campaign. German propaganda emphasized that their troops were fighting to defend their homes and families from invaders, which helped to foster high morale. (Author)

expenses by delegating certain functions down to individual units and using conscripts as a pool of labour, forcing infantry regiments to operate their own bakeries, boot makers, carpenters and other essential services. Finally, the Tsarist regime increasingly used regular infantry regiments for police duties, to guard factories or railroads during labour strikes. Furthermore, the Russian Army was increasingly nervous about the threat of military mutinies and directed that weapons should be locked up in barracks to prevent troops from accessing them, which eliminated opportunities to conduct 'dry firing' and other weapons familiarization in local training areas.

German

The recruiting system of the German Army (Deutsches Heer) was based upon territorial districts for each *Armeekorps*. XVII. Armeekorps – the parent formation of Grenadier-Regiment *König Friedrich I* (4. Ostpreußisches) Nr. 5 – was based in Danzig (now Gdansk) and recruited its personnel from the area around that city and the rural western districts of East Prussia. The Germans believed that conscripting all personnel from the same region increased unit cohesion and promoted a sense of belonging, but this method only worked well when wars were short and losses were light, so home regions did not become denuded of military-age males. In general, the peacetime Army

preferred to select recruits from rural areas, rather than cities, based upon the presumption that 'country boys' were more accustomed to hard work and life outdoors. German males typically began their military service aged 20, but the pool of available manpower greatly exceeded the needs of the Stehendes Heer (Standing Army) in peacetime. In 1913, only 23 per cent of able-bodied males were conscripted into the Stehendes Heer; the remainder were placed either in the Reserve, the Landsturm (militia) or recycled for the next year. Thereafter, all able-bodied males served part-time in the Reserve and Landwehr until aged 45, with liability for recall upon mobilization. Of those conscripted into the Stehendes Heer, about 70 per cent were selected for the infantry, which entailed a two-year service obligation. About one-fifth of new recruits were young men with higher education who volunteered for active service in peacetime (*Einjährig-Freiwilliger*), in order to choose their own unit; these volunteers were only required to serve one year. When war was declared in August 1914, the Stehendes Heer was flooded with patriotic volunteers – called *Kriegs-Freiwilliger* – but these men would not reach the front until November 1914.

New recruits were conscripted every spring and reported to a regimental depot, where they were medically certified. Once deemed fit for service, recruits took the oath of service to the Kaiser and the Fatherland in a mass ceremony and then were issued uniforms and equipment at battalion level. The first few months of military life focused on instilling military discipline in the new recruit and physical training – the German Army did not want to begin basic training until the recruits had been well prepared. During this period, some recruits were sent back home to assist with the summer harvests, but others were kept with the regiment to assist with various labour tasks. Basic training began in October when the new recruits were formally assigned to a regular infantry company; each company received about 80 recruits, joining the other 160 existing troops in the unit. Training focused on individual-level tasks for the first five months, beginning with drill and physical training, then moving to weapons familiarization and field exercises in late December. After two years of service in the infantry, most soldiers opted to leave the Stehendes Heer and revert to the Reserve, where they only had an obligation to report for two weeks' training during annual summer field training. During out-processing, German conscripts were given mementos of their service, such as engraved beer mugs and other personal items; when taken home, these items helped to foster the idea among other young males that military service was a rite of passage. Soldiers who demonstrated leadership potential might be offered the chance to pursue a Reserve officer's commission or to remain on active service as career soldiers (*Kapitulanten*).

A typical German infantryman, probably a recalled Reservist, in 1914. I. Reservekorps was formed in Königsberg in the first days of August 1914 and quickly outfitted for action. Although the Landwehrkorps was also formed, a number of Landwehr units were detached to defend border towns and some remained to garrison the fortifications in Königsberg. One typical example of a *Landwehrmann* who served in 8. Armee was Adolf Reimer, a Berliner who had joined the Army as a volunteer in 1904 aged 21, and served in a Berlin-based *Füsilier-Regiment* for two years. Assigned to the Reserve in 1906, Reimer participated in summer manoeuvres that lasted 27 days in August 1908 and 13 days in August 1911. In 1912, he was assigned to the Landwehr and spent 13 days on manoeuvres in August that year. Although a number of authors have attempted to depict the German Reserve and Landwehr as being nearly as well trained as regular troops, it is clear that Reimer participated in only three major field exercises in the eight years before 1914, and on each occasion, he trained with a different regiment; when he was mobilized on 4 August 1914, he was assigned to Landwehr-Infanterie-Regiment Nr. 3, a unit in which he had not previously served. Reimer would fight for three years on the Eastern Front, including Göritten and the second battle of the Masurian Lakes, before being captured by the Russians in July 1917. (Nik Cornish at www.stavka.org.uk)

This Russian *ryadovoy* is about 23 years old, with two years of peace-time service under his belt. He is a Russian and comes from peasant stock. He has been accustomed to a life of living out of doors and in deprivation, so the first few months of the campaign have not caused him unusual hardship. He is illiterate and does not understand why the war has occurred, but does what he is told. As a lowly private, he will fight in a 12-man rifle squad, under the direct supervision of a *yefreitor* (corporal).

Weapons, dress and equipment

The Russian Army had learned a great deal about field uniforms after the 1904–05 Russo-Japanese War and tried to simplify their soldier's kit to the maximum extent possible by dispensing with decorative items and unnecessary luxuries. This soldier is armed with the bolt-action 7.62mm M1891 Mosin-Nagant rifle (**1**) and wears the *papaha* (**2**), a cap of natural fleece or artificial astrakhan lambswool. In colder weather the *bashlyk*, a shawl-like cowl, was also worn. The Russian Army shifted to khaki-coloured uniforms even before the end of the Russo-Japanese War; over his loose-fitting *gymnastiorka* shirt, which came in a woollen version for winter, this man wears his *shinel*, or greatcoat (**3**). There are no external buttons or other decorative items which can snag on forest undergrowth or branches. However, regimental shoulder straps (**4**) are attached onto the *shinel*; these were reversible, with one side in khaki (shown here) and the other in

brigade colour (red for 1st Brigade, blue for 2nd Brigade). The regimental number is shown in yellow on the straps, along with any rank insignia (in red for NCOs). The red collar patch (**5**) denotes the first regiment of the division; the second, third and fourth regiments wore blue, white and green respectively.

The Russian infantryman had a significantly lighter marching kit than his German opponent. This man carries 30 rounds of rifle ammunition in each of his two leather cartridge pouches (**6**). He also carries a small haversack (**7**) and an aluminium water bottle (**8**) over his right shoulder plus an entrenching tool (**9**) attached to his leather waist belt. Inside the haversack, the soldier carried rations, extra foot wrappings and 40 extra rounds of ammunition. The soldier wears the loose-fitting knee boots (**10**), which proved to be comfortable in summer and well suited for winter campaigning.

UNIFORMS, EQUIPMENT AND RATIONS

Russian

The Russian Army in World War I is typically depicted as poorly armed and under-resourced, but the Russian first-line infantry units that invaded East Prussia in August 1914 were outfitted in practical uniforms that were well suited to active campaigning in summer or winter, and fully equipped with the latest infantry weapons, of good quality. Russian infantrymen were issued the loose-fitting M1912 *gymnastiorka* tunic, which came in a cotton version for summer and a woollen version for winter. Unlike the German infantrymen, the Russian infantrymen were provided with proper winter gear, including thick overcoats, hats and felt boots – the Russian Army could operate in any weather. The Russian khaki-coloured uniform proved to be well adapted for concealing troops in the forests of Eastern Europe. While the Russian soldier's cap provided no more protection from shellfire than the German *Pickelhaube*,

Russian reservists heading to the East Prussian border by train, August 1914. Russian mobilization went fairly smoothly in terms of moving troops to the front, but the supplies necessary to support them had not been stockpiled in forward areas. (Author)

A Russian infantry regiment on the march, with officers in the foreground. Note the supply wagons on the road in the background. The Russian infantrymen marched into East Prussia with 120 rounds of rifle ammunition each, but they and their supporting machine guns and artillery quickly found that their support units had great difficulty pushing resupply forward. Most of the support went to bringing up fodder for the horses, not rations or ammunition for the infantry. Further complicating matters, the Russian Ministry of War had failed to stock the General Staff's recommended ammunition basic loads, so Rennenkampf's army was only issued 850 rounds for each field gun and a few thousand rounds for each machine gun, with little reserve left in the supply depots in the Vilna Military District. Once the campaign got going in earnest, Rennenkampf's First Army was reduced to a hand-to-mouth existence, awaiting trains from St Petersburg that then had to be moved forward on horse-drawn supply columns. In contrast, 8. Armee started the campaign with much larger ammunition stockpiles and ready access to rapid resupply by rail. Thus, the command-and-control deficiencies, when combined with the inadequate logistical support, greatly reduced the combat effectiveness of Russian infantry regiments in the early stages of the invasion of East Prussia. (Courtesy of the Central Museum of the Armed Forces, Moscow via Stavka)

it was lighter and offered some protection from the sun. Russian boots were made loose-fitting, so that troops could stuff straw in them in winter. Rather than carrying a bulky knapsack like his German counterparts, the Russian infantryman carried his rolled tent cloth and overcoat in horseshoe fashion over his shoulder. One exception to the practical nature of the Russian infantry uniform was in the continued use of *portyanki* (foot wrappings), instead of stockings. It took conscripts up to a month to learn to wear *portyanki* properly and blisters were common (of note, the Russian Army continued to issue *portyanki* to conscripts until 2008!).

At the beginning of World War I, the Russian infantry enjoyed a dull, if plentiful, diet. Russian field rations usually consisted of cabbage soup or *borscht* (beets), *kasha* (porridge) and rye bread. Like the Germans, the Russians had mobile field kitchens. Extra rations and ammunition were carried in the company supply wagon, not on soldiers' backs. Ammunition – shortages of which would become a problem in 1915 – was available in adequate quantities in the Vilna Military District warehouses, although transporting it to forward units could be a problem. Although the Russian Army had been provided with some first-rate infantry weapons, the Ministry of War had not made realistic plans to stockpile adequate ammunition for protracted operations. In 1908, the General Staff had drawn up a plan, based upon usage rates from the Russo-Japanese War, to stockpile 3 billion rounds of 7.62mm small-arms ammunition: this meant 1,000 rounds per Mosin-Nagant rifle and 75,000 rounds per machine gun. However, the Ministry of War never fully funded this plan and only 2.5 billion rounds had been stockpiled by 1914. Furthermore, Russian industry was not configured to keep up with wartime demand. There were three Russian ammunition plants and their combined annual output was estimated to be 50 million rounds per month – which proved to be woefully inadequate. Russian industry was not capable of rapid expansion and it would not be until late 1916 that ammunition output even approached demand. Consequently, the Russian infantry went to war with their basic load of ammunition but once this was spent, they would suffer from *patronnyy golod* ('cartridge hunger'). Poor logistics support would gradually sap the combat potential of Russian infantrymen.

German

German infantrymen went to war in 1914 wearing the M1907/10 *Feldgrau* uniform, which helped to conceal them on the battlefield, but it was a uniform that still exhibited parade-ground frills such as the row of brass buttons on the tunic and decorative bayonet knots. The leather M1895 Pickelhaube helmet was a ridiculous contraption that also demonstrated an affinity for decoration, but which offered no practical protection to the wearer's head. While the German infantryman's uniform was appropriate for summer campaigning in Central Europe, it was not well suited to the conditions of winter warfare on the Eastern Front. The hobnailed boots conducted cold into the wearer's feet and the M1908 overcoat was unlined and offered little defence against freezing temperatures. Yet the German Army did not anticipate much winter campaigning, and instead preferred to spend its money on training and barracks facilities. One unique feature in the Prussian Army was the issuing of identification tags for each soldier – the first of any army. The other national components in the German Army (Bavarian, Saxon and Württemberg) did not yet have ID tags. Nevertheless, the German Army's pre-war uniforms were overly complex and by 1915 substantial changes were underway to make them more suitable for the reality of combat.

German infantrymen were rather well-fed and required about 1.4kg of rations per day, primarily bread, meat and vegetables. This meant that a full-strength infantry regiment consumed about 4.6 tonnes of food per day – a not insignificant amount. An infantry division, with its large number of horses in the artillery and support units, required about 60 tonnes of rations and fodder per day, meaning that operations could not be conducted very far from friendly railheads. As long as German regiments operated within East Prussia, they could rely upon their excellent rail networks to keep them in supply, but this advantage disappeared once they crossed the border into Lithuania. Even an infantry battalion had a fairly large support organization

A German infantry unit pausing during the march. Note that the troops are wearing their soft caps, so contact is probably not expected. The German infantryman's load was increased to about 30kg by the addition of an 11kg backpack to carry additional clothing, rations and ammunition; this was of questionable necessity given that in East Prussia they were operating on friendly soil and close to supply bases. (Nik Cornish at www.stavka.org.uk)

with 19 wagons and 58 horses; four ammunition wagons, one medical wagon and four mobile field kitchens (known as the *Gulaschkanonen*) in the *Gefechtstroß* (combat trains) and five baggage and five supply wagons in the *Gepäcktroß* (field trains). Although the Germans had greatly improved their tactical feeding methods, the staple of the German infantry – bread – could not be baked on the move, which meant that logistical sustainment could not really keep up with a war of manoeuvre.

Each regimental machine-gun detachment required a great deal of support, including three ammunition wagons and four other wagons, pulled by 45 horses – this was a great deal of effort to get just six MG 08s into action. Altogether, the German infantry regiment's support elements included 65 wagons and 235 horses.

German artillery and field kitchens follow the infantry. While the German infantry were capable of marching 30–40km per day, their support troops had difficulty keeping up. In particular, field kitchens needed to remain in place for some time to bake bread – a vital component of the German infantryman's daily requirement. (Nik Cornish at www.stavka.org.uk)

LEADERSHIP AND COMMUNICATIONS

Russian

Most Russian infantry officers in First Army had begun their military training aged 14–15 with three years of study at the 'Yunker' school (*Yunkerskiye uchilishcha*) in Vilna, Moscow or St Petersburg. Afterwards, a Yunker went on to one of a dozen military schools, such as the Vilenskoe Military School in Vilna (*Vilenskoe Voennoe Uchilishche*), the Alexander Military School in Moscow or the Vladimirskoe Military School in St Petersburg. After 2–3 years of focused study and drill, these cadets could apply for a commission. Contrary to the perception that all officers in the Russian Imperial Army came from aristocratic backgrounds, in fact more than one-third came from peasant or lower class origins and the military offered the chance for social advancement. Those cadets from aristocratic backgrounds usually went into the cavalry or Guards units, but the majority of Russian infantry officers in 1914 were from more humble backgrounds. A good number – including Rennenkampf, 10. Armee commander General ot infanterii Baron Thaddeus von Sievers (1853–1915) and General-mayor Arthur S.E. Beymelburg, a brigade commander in 27th Infantry Division – came from ethnic German origins. Although these men gained some respectability as officers, they did not enjoy the status that Prussian officers enjoyed and were only paid one-quarter of their German opposite numbers.

Although Russian leaders at regimental level and below knew their trade fairly well after spending decades in the same units, in general, officers were not adept at training troops. Instead, most of the training was conducted by non-commissioned officers (NCOs), but there were too few veteran NCOs to train all the recruits so the Russian Army instituted a 'buddy system' at company level, whereby experienced enlisted men were paired with a 'rookie', the idea being for each experienced man to pass on his knowledge to a soldier

Russian officers at a rail mobilization area during the early days of World War I. Relations between Russian officers and their enlisted troops have generally been characterized as very poor but that is based upon the erroneous assumption that most officers came from aristocratic backgrounds, yet this was not always true. Enlisted soldiers were required to address officers as 'your honour', but in regiments where the officers came from lower-class backgrounds there was more likely to be a paternalistic-style relationship among pre-war regulars. Influenced by the French, Russian officers believed that morale was the most critical factor on the battlefield and many made a concerted effort in the pre-war units to build as much *esprit de corps* as possible. Consequently, wartime accounts indicate that the Russian first-line infantry units at the beginning of the war had far more unit cohesion than those raised in 1915–16. Even so, many Russian officers paid little attention to the needs or attitudes of their enlisted troops, and relations between officers and soldiers would deteriorate steadily during the war, to reach a breaking point in 1917. (Nik Cornish at www. stavka.org.uk)

A natty-looking group of Russian infantry officers. One of the main problems with the Russian Army was that they had too few trained junior officers and when they began to suffer casualties, they had to replace them with almost untrained reserve officers or promote one of their scarce NCOs. In contrast, the Germans had invested more in their Reserve cadres and had no shortage of competent NCOs. By mid-1915, the Russian Army would be forced to draft candidates for reserve-officer training from the ranks of lawyers, clerks, tradesmen – anyone with some literacy and management abilities – and then rush them through a few months of training and ship them off to the front. These kind of *Ersatz* officers lacked institutional loyalty to the Russian Army as well as the inability to earn the respect of their men. The hastily trained reserve officers could not hold their battered units together like the old experienced pre-war regular officers, so discipline within the Russian Army began to disintegrate. (Courtesy of the Central Museum of the Armed Forces, Moscow via Stavka)

of the next year group before mustering out. However, the Russian Army's lack of a large pool of competent, career NCOs was a serious deficiency; whereas a pre-war German infantry company typically had 12 career NCOs, a Russian infantry company was fortunate if it had two.

Yet the real problem with the Russian officer corps lay in the reserve officer ranks and in the most senior ranks. The Russian Army started the war with a severe shortage of junior officers and had to immediately commission a large number of officer cadets during the mobilization phase. Relatively few reserve commissions had been granted before the war and little funding provided for their development. Virtually all of the reserve officers who arrived at their units during General Mobilization were inadequately trained and incapable of leading troops into battle. Once combat losses began to eliminate the pre-war regular officers wholesale, the reservists were forced to play an increasingly important role as the war dragged on. The situation at the top was just as bad, due to the tendency of Tsar Nicholas II to place incompetent court favourites in high-ranking positions, from corps- to army-level commands. Furthermore, most of the better senior commanders went to the Galician Front to fight the Austrians, leaving First and Tenth armies with a large proportion of incompetent or mediocre commanders. Russian senior officers were more like military administrators, with little understanding of battlefield realities.

Both the Russian and German armies had similar limitations with battlefield communications, which made effective reconnaissance difficult.

This *Gefreiter* is approximately 28 years old. He is in good health and not yet suffering from the effects of prolonged fatigue and living outdoors. He is confident that the war will be over soon and has been promoted due to his demonstrated competence as an infantryman. Normally, a *Gefreiter* would lead one of the infantry company's eight nine-man *Gruppen*, but he could also serve as a runner for platoon leader or be assigned other special tasks such as leading an ammunition resupply detail.

Weapons, dress and equipment

This soldier, equivalent to a lance corporal, is armed with the bolt-action 7.92mm Gew 98 rifle (**1**); he wears the M1895 leather Pickelhaube helmet (**2**), with his regiment's number marked in green on the cloth cover. The German Army adopted the *Feldgrau* uniform in 1907, a fairly 'dressy' uniform for combat, with shiny brass buttons and red piping – most of these decorative features would disappear on German uniforms issued in 1916. In colder weather, though, the M1908 greatcoat (**3**) was worn; single-breasted, with six brass buttons, it featured shoulder-straps (**4**) with corps-colour edging and the regimental number or cipher in red.

This soldier wears the M1895 knapsack (**5**), with his shelter half (**6**) rolled on the top side and mess tin (**7**) strapped on the back. Inside

the knapsack, he carries his reserve rations, a toiletry kit, low-quarter shoes, an extra shirt, tent poles, extra ammunition, his soft cap and a song book! Adding to this noise-making, uncomfortable collection of accoutrements, the German infantryman wore his aluminium water bottle (**8**) and cloth ration bag (**9**) on his right hip. On his left hip, he carries his entrenching tool and bayonet (**10**) with decorative knot. He carries a total of 120 rounds of ammunition in his six leather cartridge pouches (**11**). Finally, in an era when there were few trucks or other forms of mechanized transport, the most important part of the marching infantry's kit was his leather marching boots (**12**). It is noteworthy that this was the one item of kit that the German Army had not updated in nearly fifty years.

Although both armies used wire for telephone communications while on the defence, this was less possible on the offence and even if the corps or division command post was wired in, the regimental-level scouts up front were not. Consequently, there could be considerable delays in forwarding information obtained by scouts via messengers back to their command elements. Furthermore, anyone who has worked with scouts knows the frustration of constantly pulling for more detail on an initial contact report – how many? Heading which direction? What weapons, etc.? The lack of real-time communications links between command elements and their forward eyes and ears created a debilitating 'Fog of War' at times which rendered tactical decision-making problematic.

German

Prussian infantry officers enjoyed considerable social status but they were paid relatively little and promoted very slowly. In peacetime, it would take about ten years to reach the rank of *Hauptmann* to command an infantry company and 25 years to be promoted to *Major* and attain battalion command. Marriage was unattainable for most of the first decade of service. The Prussian officer corps was extremely homogenous in terms of their Lutheran faith, secondary-school education and minor aristocracy-endowed social status, and these men were carefully selected by regimental commanders. Boys usually entered a *Kadettenanstalt* (cadet school) aged 13 to begin their preparation for a military career. These cadet schools were expensive, costing up to 900 Marks per year, which excluded much of the emerging middle class. Elite aspirants, usually the scions of former Prussian generals, went to the Prussian *Hauptkadettenanstalt* at Groß-Lichterfelde in Berlin. Aged 19 or so, the aspirant could apply to join an infantry regiment as a *Fahnenjunker* (officer cadet) and if selected, could receive a commission within about six months. After about eight years of service as a company-grade officer in an infantry regiment, a promising officer could apply for higher-level military training at the Prussian Kriegsakademie in Berlin, although only one applicant in five was accepted. Graduation from the Kriegsakademie's rigorous three-year course was the pathway to the Großer Generalstab and senior command. The German Army sought to create well-rounded officers, adept at both field command and staff work, who were trained to be aggressive problem-solvers. However, very few Prussian officers bothered to study Russian or learn much about the Russian Army – primarily due to anti-Slavic racist prejudices – even though this force was the likely opponent of troops stationed in East Prussia.

The heart and soul of the German Army was its professional NCO corps, made up of long-service soldiers. The German NCO was the primary trainer and tactical leader within the infantry company and such men's high personal standards ensured that the unit was ready for combat. German infantry tactics were aided by these NCOs, who were trained to exercise initiative on the battlefield and who were capable of leading advances without officers. Most German NCOs were trained within their regiment, but large garrison towns like Danzig also offered specialized courses to sharpen NCO skills for training marksmanship or operating machine guns. These NCOs generally spent their whole career in the same regiment and if they went to the Reserves, they usually remained affiliated with this regiment for semi-annual training. At the start of the war, each German infantry platoon would normally be commanded by a junior officer but as casualties mounted in 1914, NCOs would increasingly be placed in charge of leading tactical sub-units.

Instead of having battalion- or regimental-level scouts as the Russians did, German infantry divisions started the war with an organic cavalry regiment; this meant that the division could deploy a screen of 300–400 mounted cavalry troops along its expected avenue of advance. However, reconnaissance skills at the start of World War I were not particularly good, especially in terms of accurate reporting. Mounted scouts were more likely to provide general observations such as 'enemy ahead', rather than detailed and useful information such as 'enemy company-size infantry unit entrenched in the next village'. Communications at company level relied upon eight bicycle-equipped messengers, although the main idea was that a company commander could keep the majority of his troops within eyesight so that they could respond to verbal commands and hand signals. Directing infantry in combat under fire at the battalion level was extremely difficult and could involve a substantial time lag between commands being issued and being received by all sub-units.

TACTICS, WEAPONS AND TRAINING

Russian

Combat experience in the Russo-Japanese War had taught the Russian Army the value of machine guns, barbed wire and entrenchments, which were incorporated into the updated Russian tactical doctrine developed during the period 1906–14. In particular, the Russian infantry were taught to avoid

Russian infantry, probably in pre-war manoeuvres. Russian infantry tactics were generally oriented towards the defence. Note how the company is deployed on line and the officers standing to observe. In real combat, these officers would rapidly have attracted enemy fire. Although the Russian infantry had begun developing new 'bounding tactics' with small groups of infantry prior to the war, they lacked sufficient trained NCO squad leaders to lead these kind of advances. Instead, the Russians still relied on 'chain' tactics, which was essentially advancing in successive platoon-size skirmisher lines, because these could be controlled by company-level officers. If the officers were killed or wounded, though, the Russian infantry was not trained to exercise small-unit initiative. (Author)

The Mosin-Nagant M1891 had been in service with the Russian Army for over two decades and battle-tested in the Russo-Japanese War. A new bullet was introduced in 1908 with a lighter, streamlined shape. Combat experience led to improvements in the weapon's sights and made it sturdier and easier to handle. By 1914, the Mosin-Nagant was a proven, reliable weapon and trained infantrymen could use it to engage targets out to 500m. The Mosin-Nagant had a slower rate of fire than the German rifle and a significant recoil, but it stood the test of combat quite well. (© Royal Armouries XII.2663)

massed formations that drew hostile artillery fire and an effort was made to improve marksmanship training. A number of Russian infantry officers embraced the new concept of 'fire tactics' based upon the massed firepower of rifles, machine guns and field artillery, although this was by no means universal.

The primary infantry weapon of the Russian Army in 1914 was the bolt-action Mosin-Nagant M1891 rifle, also known as the 'Three Line Rifle', which fired 7.62×54mmR ammunition from a five-round detachable stripper clip. In addition, the Russian Army had developed a practical hand grenade in 1912 and an improved model, the M1914 hand grenade (*Ruchnaya granata obraztsa 1914 goda*), was issued just prior to the start of the war. This was the only hand grenade in service with infantrymen at the start of the conflict (although British engineers and German *Pioniere* (combat engineers) had hand grenades). Interestingly, the Russian Army had begun work on developing a semi-automatic rifle right after the Russo-Japanese War ended and by 1911 this research was beginning to bear fruit; in 1916, Russia would introduce the Fedorov Avtomat, a 6.5mm automatic rifle. Yet the Russian Army did not have adequate ammunition even for its bolt-action rifles and its leadership was opposed to automatic weapons since they feared that troops would expend all their ammunition in the first action.

The main Russian infantry-support weapon was the water-cooled 7.62mm Maxim Model 1910 machine gun (*Pulemyot Maxima*), usually mounted on a Sokolov carriage. The Russian Army had received its first Maxims in 1901 and it was the first European army to purchase a large number of the new weapons. During the Russo-Japanese War, the Russian Army gained considerable combat experience with machine guns in Manchuria, although the weapons were still mounted on artillery-style carriages. After that war, the Russian Army ordered modifications to the basic Maxim and by 1910 they had a much-improved version that was less prone to stoppages. Usually, the men in the machine-gun detachment were hand-picked from the best soldiers in the regiment. Russian machine-gun detachments received 50,000 rounds for training each year, which was only half as much as their German counterparts, but had significant advantages in terms of mobility and combat experience. Russian infantry commanders were very aggressive about pushing their machine guns forward, even in the offence.

The pre-war Army put considerable emphasis upon rifle marksmanship and recruits were trained to engage both stationary and moving targets out to 1,400m. Traditionalists within the Army continued to speak of the value of

the bayonet charge – a belief that was endorsed in other armies as well – and to reinforce this ideal, Russian infantrymen were ordered to leave their bayonets fixed at all times upon their Mosin-Nagant rifles. Unlike the Germans, the Russian placed considerable emphasis during infantry training on hand-to-hand and close-quarter combat, arising from lessons learned in the trenches around Port Arthur in 1904–05. Russian infantry field training also emphasized entrenching, during both offensive and defensive operations, which was another tactical lesson learned during the Russo-Japanese War. Russian field manoeuvres also experimented with conducting night attacks – aspects of combat the Germans were not focused upon. The Russian Army

Russian machine-gunners employ two-man tow ropes to pull their Maxim guns. This weapon weighed 64.3kg, which was slightly less than the German MG 08, and it could be pulled into action by two men. It was fed by 250-round belts and could fire up to 600 rounds per minute; in combat, each machine-gun crew was provided with 2,000 rounds of ammunition. The weapon was better adapted for field mobility than the German MG 08. Extra ammunition was carried in the detachment's supply wagon. (Author)

Russian infantry in the attack through a row of barbed wire, while under artillery fire. The Russian troops tended to advance slowly and cautiously compared to other armies, but they still managed to commit the sort of flag-waving, bugle-blowing catastrophes that the French Army suffered in Alsace-Lorraine in 1914. (From the fonds of the RGAKFD in Krasnogorsk via Stavka)

trained year-round, with winter and summer phases, which made the troops accustomed to the idea of operating outdoors under all conditions. Large-scale battalion-level, regiment-level and corps-level exercises were conducted during the summer months, although these manoeuvres tended to be much shorter than those conducted by German infantry units. The US military attaché in Russia, Captain Nathan K. Averill, observed the August 1912 manoeuvres at Krasnoye Selo near St Petersburg and noted the great improvement in the Russian infantry: 'The [Russian] infantry attack was a beautiful thing to watch, well coordinated, well timed and cohesive, though coming through thick woods.'

Averill also noted the extensive use of field telephones by Russian regimental- and battalion-level staffs, which improved their ability to pass orders quickly. Even so, co-ordination with neighbouring units on either flank was often very poor, exposing Russian units to enveloping attacks. At the tactical level, individual Russian infantry regiments were well-versed in the tactics of movement to contact and hasty defence, but co-ordinating the actions of four regiments was difficult for Russian division commanders and their staffs. Nor did Russian pre-war doctrine provide guidance on how to mass combat power at the decisive point on the battlefield – it was just assumed that it would happen somehow. Russian tactical doctrine was best suited for the defence, even when conducting a strategic offensive into East Prussia.

German

While the Germans lacked recent combat experience, they possessed a tactical doctrine that stressed offensive action as the solution to virtually all problems. Even though the strategic mission of 8. Armee was to defend East Prussia, it was intended to be a very active defence and prior to the war, Generaloberst Helmuth von Moltke, chief of the German *Großer Generalstab*, stated that, 'when the Russians arrive – no defense. Just attack, attack, attack'. Some Landwehr and Landsturm units were assigned purely defensive missions in border towns, but all Stehendes Heer and Reserve infantrymen were trained primarily for attack, not defence.

The primary German infantry weapon in 1914 was the bolt-action Gew 98 rifle, which fired 7.92×57mm ammunition from a five-round detachable stripper clip. Each German infantryman carried 120 rounds in his ammunition pouches, plus 30 in his pack. An infantry company usually carried an additional 70 rounds per man in its supply wagon. While the troops were issued with bayonets, the German Army no longer regarded 'cold steel' as very useful on the modern battlefield. The German Army on the Eastern Front was lower in priority than the forces deployed on the Western Front and this was particularly noticeable in terms of equipment. By March 1915, some German Reserve and Landwehr units on the Eastern Front would even begin to receive captured Mosin-Nagant rifles as replacements for lost weapons, as well as obsolete Gew 88 rifles.

While the Gew 98 had seen limited combat use during the Boxer Rebellion (1898–1900), it had not been significantly upgraded prior to World War I. The Gew 98 was equipped with simple iron sights, which limited its ability to engage targets accurately out to about 500m. A trained infantryman could fire five aimed rounds within 10–12 seconds and reload within five seconds. The weapon had a substantial 'kick' and prolonged firing could lead to bruised shoulders. (Neil Grant photograph, © Royal Armouries PR.612)

German postcard depicting a pair of MG 08 machine guns firing from a roadside ditch. These weapons are placed too close together – for ease of command and control – but eventually the Germans would learn to disperse them to avoid being easily suppressed by enemy artillery. The MG 08 was a belt-fed machine gun that could fire 400 rounds per minute and had an effective range up to 2,000m, although its practical range was about 1,000m. (Author)

By 1914, the main German infantry-support weapon was the 7.92mm Maschinengewehr 08 (MG 08), which was introduced to replace the original cumbersome Maxim design. The German Army was initially slow to embrace the machine gun since it was a heavy weapon that did not fit in well with its doctrine of mobile offensive operations. The first Maxim machine guns were purchased by the German Army in 1899, but initially only assigned to cavalry and *Jäger* units. It was not until 1905 that the German Army began to provide machine-gun detachments to its infantry regiments, but this conservative attitude changed after the effectiveness of the weapon was observed in the Russo-Japanese War. By the end of 1908, every German first-line infantry regiment had at least one six-gun battery of machine guns. Although some German Reserve infantry regiments had not yet been equipped with machine guns, three fortunate infantry regiments in I. Reservekorps in East Prussia started the war with two six-gun batteries each. Experiments conducted at annual summer manoeuvres revealed the potential of the new weapon and stoked the demand for more machine guns. In peacetime, machine-gun batteries were given 110,000 rounds of ammunition to fire annually, mostly during summer manoeuvres.

Although the Germans were aware of the offensive potential of the machine gun, they started the war with great faith in the firepower of their rifle-armed infantrymen. German tactical doctrine was codified in the *Das Exerzier-Reglement für die Infanterie*, issued in May 1906. This document focused entirely on individual and company-level training, which placed great emphasis upon individual marksmanship and infantry tactics based upon achieving 'fire superiority' over an opponent. Recruits were also taught individual-movement techniques to use cover and concealment to move tactically. This approach meant that infantry had to advance in fairly cohesive groups in order for one junior officer to direct and mass each group's firepower, hence German infantry in August 1914 is often depicted in dense marching clusters; in combat, these clusters would spread out into skirmish lines. While German doctrine specified moving to the battlefield in column, then

switching to skirmish lines when within 1km or less of the enemy, in practice German commanders were reluctant to deploy into linear formations too soon, since this meant that command devolved from regimental commanders down to platoon leaders and company commanders. In contrast, Russian infantry had learned to spread out in Manchuria and they continued to use these tactics freely in East Prussia, although this made it more difficult for commanders to control their formations.

The annual training calendar saw German infantrymen training in successively larger units and formations. In early February, recruits were assessed and those who passed were assigned permanent positions in the company, which then began a six-week period of company-level training. In mid-March, the unit progressed to two weeks of battalion-level training. Although issued entrenching tools, German infantry recruits were not given many opportunities to practise digging fighting positions, since it clashed with the offensive-oriented doctrine. Large-scale unit training was conducted during the summer months, with regimental- and divisional-level field exercises in manoeuvre-training areas in East Prussia. The culmination of the annual training cycle was the corps-level manoeuvres, conducted in September with up to three *Armeekorps*. The *Kaisermänover* (Kaiser Manoeuvres), with Kaiser Wilhelm II in attendance, was an event only held in East Prussia in 1901 and 1910. This kind of large-scale unit training was useful for training senior commanders and their staffs, but it did little to enhance tactical competence at the regimental level and below. During these large-scale exercises, reservists were recalled and trained alongside first-line troops for 2–3 weeks.

Each Stehendes Heer infantry division had very strong fire support, provided by four artillery battalions, with 54 7.7cm FK 96 nA guns and 18 10.5cm FH 98/09 howitzers; these would be supplemented by corps-level 15cm sFH 02 howitzers. Capable of firing high explosive, shrapnel and smoke rounds, under ideal conditions the 7.7cm FK 96 nA could fire ten rounds per minute in a relatively flat trajectory and had an effective range of 5,500m. At the outset of the war, division-level artillery would usually be used in direct-fire engagements and its effective range under these conditions was just 4,000–5,000m. The division- and corps-level howitzers were useful for engaging targets in defilade. (Tom Laemlein / Armor Plate Press)

Gumbinnen

20 August 1914

BACKGROUND TO BATTLE

On 4 August, Rennenkampf sent a cavalry division on a raid across the East Prussian frontier near Kybartai; it discovered that most border settlements were fortified and garrisoned by detachments of Landsturm, and that elements of General der Infanterie Hermann von François' I. Armeekorps, a Stehendes Heer formation, were in the vicinity. The Russian cavalry raid alerted Prittwitz that Rennenkampf was likely to cross the East Prussian border before Samsonov's Second Army, so soon afterwards Prittwitz began deploying his XVII. Armeekorps (General der Kavallerie August von Mackensen) and I. Reservekorps (Generalleutnant, later General der Infanterie, Otto von Below) to reinforce François near Insterburg. The Germans had fortified the area in the Masurian Lakes, the so-called Angerapp-Stellung, in order to channel any Russian advance from Lithuania through the Insterburg Gap, where Prittwitz was waiting to strike the Russian vanguard. Only XX. Armeekorps (General der Artillerie Friedrich von Scholtz) was left to watch the Polish border, facing the expected avenue of approach of Samsonov's Second Army. On 10 August, the Russians mounted another cavalry raid across the border with two divisions but encountered tougher resistance south of Eydtkuhnen, and were repulsed. Three days later, Rennenkampf arrived in the Lithuanian border city of Kalvarija and set up his forward headquarters.

The rest of his army, gathering in assembly areas 30km from the frontier, was ordered to begin moving towards the East Prussian border.

At 0800hrs on the morning of 17 August, First Army began crossing into East Prussia in force. General ot infanterii Nikolai Yepanchin's 3rd Corps was deployed in the middle, along the Kovno–Königsberg railway line, while 20th Corps (General ot infanterii Vladimir V. Smirnov) covered its northern flank and 4th Corps (General ot artillerii Eris Khan Sultan Giryei Aliev) marched on its southern flank. Rennenkampf's army had no mass, as it was spread out across a 70km-wide front. Furthermore, the five cavalry divisions were poorly deployed on the army's flanks, meaning 3rd Corps had to reconnoitre to its front with its own organic Cossack regiment. Soon after crossing the border, Yepanchin's 3rd Corps encountered several fortified villages, occupied by Landwehr personnel and a few guns. At about 1100hrs, Yepanchin sent General-leytenant Pavel I. Bulgakov's 25th Infantry Division on the right to take the town of Stallupönen, while General-leytenant August-Karl M. Adaridi's 27th Infantry Division split into brigade-sized columns to seize the fortified villages of Dopönen and Göritten. Polkovnik Konstantin P. Otryganev, commander of the 106th Infantry Regiment *Ufimsky*, led his regiment in its baptism of fire at Dopönen, which the regiment succeeded in capturing. However, as the 105th Infantry Regiment *Orenburg* and the 108th Infantry Regiment *Saratov* were advancing in column towards Göritten, unknown troops appeared on their southern flank. It was assumed that these were friendly troops from 4th Corps, but they were not – they were Germans. The slower-moving 4th Corps had allowed a 15km-wide gap to open between it and the neighbouring 3rd Corps.

Prittwitz had begun assembling three of his four corps near Insterburg on 16 August, but he did not intend to mount a counter-attack until he could

Rennenkampf's First Army was often engaged by Landsturm rearguards during the initial invasion. Here, Landsturm personnel fire their Gew 88 rifles from behind a railway embankment in East Prussia, 1914. Note the bugler at the ready. (Scherl / SZ Photo)

General ot infanterii Nikolai A. Yepanchin and his 3rd Corps staff. Yepanchin was a Guards officer and General Staff trained, having also spent a great deal of time around the Tsar's court. However, he was less familiar with modern battlefield conditions and his only prior combat experience was as a junior officer in the 1877–78 Russo-Turkish War. After being relieved of command in 1915, he would flee to the West with the defeated Whites in 1920 and live out the rest of his days in France. (Author)

mass all three corps against the lead Russian corps. François, whose I. Armeekorps was already acting as a covering force behind the Landsturm-held towns, was only authorized to conduct a 'reconnaissance in force' to determine the Russian dispositions once they crossed the border. François exceeded his orders, however, and decided to launch an unauthorized spoiling attack with his corps, even though he was uncertain about the enemy's strength or dispositions. Fortune often does favour the bold and François was fortunate that he was able to strike against the exposed left flank of Yepanchin's 3rd Corps. The German troops approaching Adaridi's 27th Infantry Division were four infantry battalions and five artillery batteries from 2. Infanterie-Division, which caught the Russian infantry in march columns. The Russian artillery was still moving forward and unable to provide support in the opening moments of the battle of Stallupönen (which actually occurred south-east of Göritten). Polkovnik Petr D. Komarov's *Orenburg* Regiment was surprised, hit in the flank and literally 'mown down' by German rapid-fire volleys. Most of the damage was done by German rifle fire, not machine guns or artillery. Komarov tried to rally his shattered regiment but was killed in the action and 3,020 of his troops were killed or captured. The collapse of the *Orenburg* Regiment caused a chain reaction, which incited the unengaged 107th Infantry Regiment *Troitsky* and the *Saratov* Regiment to begin retreating back towards the border. Only the intervention of the Russian divisional artillery, General-mayor Vladimir N. Folimonov's 27th Artillery Brigade, prevented a complete rout. The Russian gunners coolly engaged the advancing enemy infantrymen with shrapnel; wisely, the Germans decided not to pursue Adaridi's broken division to the border. At this point, an angry Prittwitz ordered François to break off the unauthorized action and retire towards Gumbinnen.

After retreating back to the border, Yepanchin's 3rd Corps retraced its steps on the afternoon of 18 August and occupied Stallupönen by evening. The next day, Rennenkampf ordered his army to advance up to the eastern bank of the Rominte River, which resulted in small-scale actions against more Landsturm troops and François' rearguards. By the end of 19 August, all three Russian corps were near the Rominte, but First Army was already disorganized and suffering from logistical problems after crossing the East Prussian border. The five cavalry divisions attached to Rennenkampf's army caused an inordinate drain on his limited logistical resources, requiring priority being given to fodder for horses, not supplies for infantry units. Field bakeries were not ready to operate yet, so the infantry had no bread but were given stale

hardtack for two weeks. Initially, the Russian logistics units could not provide water, salt and a myriad of other basic supplies to Rennenkampf's troops. Samsonov's Second Army was not scheduled to begin crossing the East Prussian border until the next day, so Rennenkampf figured that he could pause to rest his forces on 20 August.

Meanwhile, François had exaggerated his success at Stallupönen and managed to convince Prittwitz to commit all three corps to counter-attack the Russians on the Rominte River.

German infantry sections in prone firing positions assumed off the line of march, August 1914. This is the kind of disposition XVII. Armeekorps initially used prior to assaulting the Russian position at Mattischkehmen. Everyone on line, then advance! (Scherl / SZ Photo)

MAP KEY

1 0600–0800hrs: 35. Infanterie-Division employs three infantry regiments to begin attacking the left flank of 25th Infantry Division.

2 0800hrs: 36. Infanterie-Division begins pushing in the outposts of 27th Infantry Division and advances upon Mattischkehmen.

3 0900–1000hrs: 71. Infanterie-Brigade mounts an attack upon Mattischkehmen but is repulsed by the 106th Infantry Regiment *Ufimsky* and the Russian artillery.

4 1100hrs: The left flank of 25th Infantry Division begins to withdraw under pressure. 71. Infanterie-Brigade uses this opportunity to mount a second attack on Mattischkehmen with the support of 70. Infanterie-Brigade, but is repulsed.

5 1300hrs: 87. Infanterie-Brigade (35. Infanterie-Division) pursues the retreating 25th Infantry Division but is hit by enfilade artillery fire from both Russian artillery groups and suffers heavy losses. The *Orenburg* Regiment continues to hold the edge of the woods.

6 1430hrs: A German probe towards Warschlegen is repulsed. A counter-attack by the 108th Infantry Regiment *Saratov* captures two German field-artillery batteries.

7 1500hrs: 27th Infantry Division commits its reserve, the 107th Infantry Regiment *Troitsky*, which counter-attacks into the flank of the over-extended 87. Infanterie-Brigade. 36. Infanterie-Division falls back 15km in disorder.

8 1500hrs: 69. Infanterie-Brigade attacks the right flank of 40th Infantry Division, which pulls back, exposing the left flank of 27th Infantry Division.

9 1715–1800hrs: Mackensen commits his corps reserve, Infanterie-Regiment *von Borcke* (4. Pommersches) Nr. 21, to make a third assault upon Mattischkehmen, but this unit is repulsed as well. After suffering heavy losses, 36. Infanterie-Division retreats.

Battlefield environment

Thursday 20 August 1914 was a partly cloudy day, with sunrise occurring around 0620hrs. Temperatures rose to 22–25 degrees Celsius by noon, with the wind blowing from the west. The Germans would be advancing eastwards, with the sun in their eyes.

The village of Mattischkehmen was surrounded by relatively flat farmland, although there were folds and small hillocks that offered some degree of cover and concealment. Late-summer crops like wheat were still evident, but the movement of troops combined with neglect for a week or more had trampled many of the fields. Between the Rominte River and Mattischkehmen, the land sloped down gently to the west, providing some dead space (free of observation) for the Germans, but this area was crossed by drainage ditches and somewhat marshy. The village consisted of about a dozen single-storey structures, some of which were built out of brick, but mostly wooden construction. Some of the buildings had been damaged by German shellfire, but not too badly yet. A substantial amount of trees and tall grass bordered the village, but there was good visibility to the west. The main dirt road, traversing from north-east to south-west, bisected the village.

North of the village, there was a very large, thick wooded area, which was held by another Russian battalion. To the south, there were more small clumps of trees and irrigation ditches. Overall, the terrain favoured a hasty defence, since the Russians were mostly deployed under cover while the Germans had to advance across 2–3km of open terrain with minimal cover.

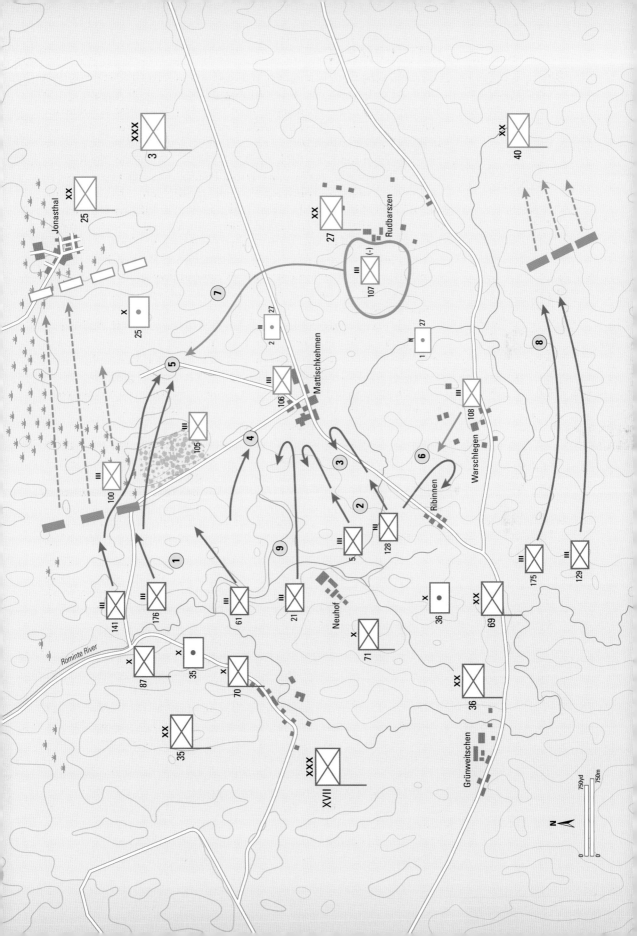

INTO COMBAT

The ensuing battle of Gumbinnen was to consist of three distinct corps-sized actions. The German counter-attack began at dawn on 20 August, against Smirnov's 20th Corps on Rennenkampf's northern flank near Gumbinnen. François was able to mass the artillery of his I. Armeekorps against 28th Infantry Division, which was not yet entrenched, while 2. Infanterie-Division manoeuvred to conduct a flank attack at 0800hrs. Once again, the Russians had not secured their flanks properly and François was able to carry out an envelopment which overwhelmed 28th Infantry Division; it routed with the loss of 7,000 of its troops. However, 20th Corps' 29th Infantry Division was able to refuse its flank and made a determined stand, which prevented François from rolling up Rennenkampf's right flank. Not only was the German artillery fire ineffective against entrenched Russian infantry, but owing to poor communications, François' own artillery accidentally fired on the advancing 2. Infanterie-Division; fratricide is commonplace in inexperienced units.

While François was attacking in the north, Mackensen's XVII. Armeekorps was behind schedule in moving up to attack Yepanchin's 3rd Corps, which was in the centre of Rennenkampf's line. Similarly, Below's I. Reserve-Korps was not able to join the battle until midday. At 1730hrs on 19 August, Mackensen's XVII. Armeekorps had moved out of its assembly areas and marched eastwards. His infantry spent the entire night marching 25km to the Rominte, not stopping for rest or meals. German reconnaissance prior to the coming battle was just as faulty as the Russians' and they made the mistake of assuming that the enemy had not yet occupied defensive positions. German aircraft were committed to reconnoitre the Rominte River area, but their reports suggested that not many Russian forces were in Mackensen's path and he chose not to send his own division-level cavalry scouts ahead to confirm this information. Instead, Mackensen's corps marched blindly forward into a void, assuming little resistance ahead. Even so, his troops were in confident mood: 'The attack order was received with jubilation that was hard to suppress, and the ammunition wagons almost stormed with shouts of "hurrah!" Finally, finally it was beginning! Night march, fatigue – now, just onwards!' (Preusser 1931: 15). Mackensen opted for a piecemeal frontal assault against Russian positions which he could not see. At 0600hrs he committed three infantry regiments from 35. Infanterie-Division massed against what he believed to be the left flank of a Russian division (it was 25th Infantry Division). Here, German artillery was able to achieve fire superiority and support a successful infantry attack against Russian troops who were not yet entrenched or fully supported by their own artillery. After three hours of combat, part of the Russian division retreated, exposing the right flank of the neighbouring 27th Infantry Division, but some units – such as 25th Infantry Division's 100th Infantry Regiment *Ostrov* – conducted solid rearguard actions.

In the centre, Polkovnik Konstantin P. Otryganev's *Ufimsky* Regiment held the fortified village of Mattischkehmen, supported by a battalion of 76.2mm guns. In just a few hours, the Russian infantry had managed to dig some shallow trenches inside the village and their artillery was well concealed in nearby woods. On the 19th Rennenkampf had directed his units to move up to the Rominte and then entrench themselves and fortify captured villages, but

Russian troops during one of the early actions in East Prussia, 1914. Although the troops are all prone, note how closely bunched together they are – enemy artillery will soon enforce dispersion. (Author)

most placed a greater priority on resting their tired troops instead of reaching their designated positions in a timely manner. One exception was provided by General-mayor Arthur S.E. Beymelburg, the commander of 2nd Infantry Brigade, 27th Infantry Division. On the night of 19/20 August, Beymelburg went on a personal reconnaissance, acting as his own quartering party, and selected positions for the division's infantry to occupy. Thanks to Beymelburg's initiative, 27th Infantry Division was able to move quickly into favourable defensive positions and begin entrenching before dawn on the morning of 20 August. The remnants of the *Orenburg* Regiment, reduced to about 1,300 men, held the woods on 27th Infantry Division's right flank. To the south, the *Saratov* Regiment held the fortified village of Warschlegen, supported by another battalion of 76.2mm guns. General-leytenant Adaridi kept the *Troitsky* Regiment in division reserve. Despite poor connections with his neighbouring divisions on either flank, Adaridi held a very good defensive position with all of his troops entrenched and clear fields of fire.

Incredibly, Mackensen initially committed only a single brigade, Oberst von Dewitz's 71. Infanterie-Brigade from 36. Infanterie-Division, to capture Mattischkehmen. This brigade consisted of Grenadier-Regiment *König Friedrich I* (4. Ostpreußisches) Nr. 5 under Oberst Hartwig Freiherr von Eichendorff and Danziger Infanterie-Regiment Nr. 128 under Oberst Edwin von Treskow. Generalleutnant Konstanz von Heineccius, commander of 36. Infanterie-Division, believed that his two regiments were going up against light enemy resistance, not a prepared defence. The Germans were violating a cardinal principle of how to fight an encounter battle, which was the importance of initially making contact with only the smallest possible forces in order to avoid surprises of this sort.

After pushing back Adaridi's outpost line, Dewitz's brigade began bounding forward towards Mattischkehmen at about 0800hrs, but had to cross a smaller water obstacle, the Schwentischke River. By 0900hrs, both German regiments were deployed to attack the town, with about a 1,500m-wide front. Initially, the German infantrymen used cover and concealment to bound forward in platoon-sized 'chain lines', but when they reached within about 1,000m of the town they formed into larger assault groups. The front line consisted of at least eight companies with close to 2,000 infantrymen, followed by a second line with another 1,000 troops and

Slaughter at Mattischkehmen

German view: After the signal to advance was given, Leutnant Kurt Hesse, a platoon leader in 7. Kompanie/Grenadier-Regiment Nr. 5, led his 70-man unit forward across open ground towards the Russian-held village of Mattischkehmen. The German infantrymen are advancing in lines that tend to coalesce together into clusters, which their officers could not prevent; when under fire, novice infantry instinctively draw closer for mutual support. At first, the Germans could bound forward from one tree line to the next, although these provided only sparse concealment and no cover from Russian artillery. Hesse later said that 'no enemy was to be seen' but that the Russian firepower cut swathes through the ranks of his company. The German infantrymen can see little more than the twinkle of machine guns, but cannot pinpoint the Russian main line of resistance. German artillery support is falling upon Mattischkehmen, but will fail to suppress the Russian defenders. After vainly surging forward another 200–300m, losing dozens of men, Hesse's company will begin to fall back. This was not the kind of battle that German infantry had been trained to expect – a nearly invisible enemy that could not be suppressed by a few volleys of 7.7cm fire.

Russian view: The soldiers of the 106th Infantry Regiment *Ufimsky* have brought several of their Maxim machine guns to the edge of the village to support a line of prone infantrymen. As the German come within about 1,000m of the village, the Russian machine guns open fire, supplemented by aimed rifle fire. The Russian infantrymen, who have been trained to fire with their bayonets fixed at all times, are loading and firing at a rapid rate. At the beginning of the war, when ammunition scarcity was not yet a factor, the Russians tended to fire off huge quantities of ammunition and here at Gumbinnen, this intense barrage will quickly break up the German attack. The Russian infantrymen in the village of Mattischkehmen had only begun to dig in before the German attack began, but they have been trained to use natural cover and are virtually invisible to the approaching Germans at this range. The German artillery fire causes some Russian troops to pause and look to the rear, but the artillery barrage is not very effective. With good cover and plentiful ammunition, the Russian defence is steady.

a third with 1,500 – a total of nearly 5,000 infantrymen. Yet only a few batteries of German 7.7cm guns had been deployed in time to support the attack and these guns had little effect on the *Ufimsky* Regiment, which was partly entrenched in Mattischkehmen. The German gunners were firing a mix of high-explosive and shrapnel rounds, but the 7.7cm shells had only very small bursting charges, which were designed more for engaging troops in the open than in covered terrain. Nor were any German machine guns initially in a position to support the attack, since they were too far back.

At the signal '*Los!*' ('Off!' or 'Go!') the German infantry from both regiments surged forward in thick lines towards Mattischkehmen. Leutnant Kurt Hesse, a platoon leader in 7. Kompanie of Grenadier-Regiment Nr. 5 on the left of the brigade, was one of the junior officers leading the assault:

> The units of the Grenadier-Regiment 5 came under Russian fire immediately after crossing the valley of the River Schwentischke. It was like hell opening out before us … No enemy was to be seen; nothing but the fire of thousands of rifles, of machineguns and artillery… Units quickly thinned out. Whole ranks already lay dead. Groans and cries resounded over the whole field. Our artillery was late in opening fire; urgent requests were sent by the infantry units for the artillery to come into action. (Hesse 1922: 41)

However, Hesse noted that the dug-in Russian artillery knocked out some of the German artillery limbers as they came into action and here, it was the Russians who achieved fire superiority:

> The infantry were held to the ground by the Russian fire; the men lay with their faces to the ground, no one daring to so much as raise his head, not to speak of firing a shot himself. It was the same picture in the 128th Regiment. The village of Ribinnen was taken by them, but then a storm of fire broke over them, and very soon the regiment reported that its strength was spent. (Hesse 1922: 41)

Hesse's account indicates that German tactical doctrine – which called for infantrymen caught within the enemy's beaten zone to return aimed fire to suppress the defence – was unrealistic under these kind of conditions. Even if German infantrymen could see the muzzle flashes of the Russian Maxim machine guns, the crews were protected by armoured gun shields while the

A German infantry company in the attack, 1914. Note how bunched up the troops are, with one section blending into the next, and there is no indication of bounding overwatch tactics. This is a target-rich environment and Mackensen's attack at Mattischkehmen probably appeared much like this. These troops are about to learn what machine guns can accomplish in a matter of seconds. (Author)

Hartwig Freiherr von Eichendorff

Commander of Grenadier-Regiment Nr. 5 in August 1914, Oberst Hartwig Freiherr von Eichendorff (1860–1944) came from an old Prussian aristocratic family that had settled in Silesia. Although Hartwig's father had served in the Prussian Army, his grandfather was a well-known poet and novelist from the early 19th century. Furthermore, the Eichendorffs were Catholic and the Prussian Army was a bastion of Lutheranism. Nevertheless, Hartwig followed in his father's path; he joined the Prussian Army as a cadet and was then commissioned in October 1879. He spent the next three decades in a succession of infantry assignments, slowly rising to command a company, then a battalion stationed in East Prussia. Two years prior to the war's outbreak, Eichendorff was given command of Grenadier-Regiment Nr. 5 in East Prussia and he remained in command of the regiment through the first two years of the war on the Eastern Front.

Apparently, Eichendorff was competent, but he was no career climber. In June 1916 he was promoted to *Generalmajor* and put in charge of a brigade; in April 1917 he was given command of 47. Reserve-Division. With the war in the East winding down after the fall of the Tsar, Generalmajor von Eichendorff's division was transferred to the Western Front in May 1917 and he led it into action during the *Kaiserschlacht* in March 1918. Exhausted after four years of front-line leadership, in August 1918 Eichendorff handed over the division to return home for a rest, but received no further commands before the Armistice. Eichendorff was fortunate to survive World War I and, approaching 60, he was retired in the post-war demobilization. Afterwards, he returned to Silesia and lived quietly until he died in April 1944 – just as another Russian army was advancing into the Reich.

Soldiers from Eichendorff's regiment, Grenadier-Regiment *König Friedrich I* (4. Ostpreußisches) Nr. 5, based in Danzig a few years before World War I, wearing the old Prussian blue uniform. Note the cloth coloured bands on some helmets, indicating that these troops were probably involved in a field training exercise. (Author)

German infantrymen had no cover. Pinned under enemy fire at a range of 700–800m, the German infantrymen could not mass fires as their tactical doctrine required and instead focused on survival. Digging in might have helped but one overly aggressive *Hauptmann* insisted that, 'Prussian infantry does not entrench!' German doctrine said attack, not dig in. He urged his men to get up and advance, but more troops were cut down and the advance was halted. Now the Russian machine-gunners had the German infantry pinned and could not be suppressed. Unable to advance and suffering heavy casualties, the two German infantry regiments fell back to regroup.

By 1100hrs, however, the left flank of 25th Infantry Division was beginning to falter and Mackensen ordered 35. Infanterie-Division to support a second attack upon Mattischkehmen with 70. Infanterie-Brigade. Nevertheless, the *Ufimsky* Regiment and its supporting artillery still had plenty of ammunition and the second attempt was repulsed as well. The German 7.7cm guns could not suppress the Russian defences in the town and the 15cm corps-level howitzers did not get into action until 1400hrs; when the 15cm howitzers opened fire, their first barrage landed squarely on top of

Konstantin P. Otryganev

Commander of the 106th Infantry Regiment *Ufimsky* since 8 February 1914, Konstantin Otryganev (1861–1915) was born to a well-off family in Georgia and educated at home. He joined the Russian Army aged 18. After spending two years training to be an officer at the Tiflis Infantry Cadet School, he was commissioned as a *podporuchik* (second lieutenant) in 1884 and assigned to the 162nd Infantry Regiment *Akhaltsykhskii* in Georgia. Within a few years, Otryganev was able to move into division-level staff assignments and during the 1904–05 Russo-Japanese War he served on the staff of Second Manchurian Army. In December 1910, he was promoted to *polkovnik* and assigned to command the 3rd Battalion in the *Ufimsky* Regiment.

Otryganev proved to be an aggressive infantryman who believed in leading from the front

and he distinguished himself during the invasion of East Prussia at Stallupönen and Gumbinnen. Available information suggests that he ran a tight regiment and was respected by his troops. In February 1915, Otryganev was badly wounded in the knee while leading the remnants of his regiment in the break-out attempt at Mahartse. He was captured shortly thereafter and his leg was amputated in a German field hospital. However, the operation left him very weak and he died of his wounds after only a month in captivity. Otryganev was a brave and capable infantry leader, demonstrating that at the tactical level, the Russian Army was a formidable opponent.

Polkovnik Konstantin P. Otryganev. (Author)

Grenadier-Regiment Nr. 5, causing casualties. From the German point of view, this was not the way that a battle was supposed to unfold.

Mackensen made an attempt to outflank Mattischkehmen by using Generalmajor Johannes von Hahn's 87. Infanterie-Brigade (35. Infanterie-Division) to exploit the growing gap between 25th and 27th Infantry divisions, but this brigade marched into a vicious crossfire that was not unlike the 'valley of death' at Balaklava 60 years earlier; the attempt to envelop stalled. German efforts to capture the woods north of Mattischkehmen failed when the *Orenburg* Regiment held firm and delivered steady fire into the German flanking attempt. Amazingly, a regiment that had suffered 75 per cent losses at Stallupönen only three days earlier now proved solid and

A Russian infantry strongpoint under German artillery fire, 1914. The Russians were quick to deploy barbed wire once the war in the East began to enter a positional phase, but the density of obstacle belts was never equivalent to what was found on the Western Front. (Author)

reliable. Indeed, the performance of the *Orenburg* Regiment demonstrates the rugged durability of Russian infantry units at the outset of World War I, before material shortages and political agitation had sapped their fighting spirit.

Failing to storm Mattischkehmen, Dewitz re-directed Infanterie-Regiment Nr. 128 against Warschlegen and boldly brought up two 7.7cm batteries in the open to support the attack. However, the Russian infantry and machine-gunners of the *Saratov* Regiment drove off the German infantry, while the Russian artillery suppressed the German gunners before they could get into action. Adding insult to injury, the *Saratov* Regiment mounted a local counter-attack that captured all 12 German artillery pieces, which deprived Dewitz of a good part of his fire support. During the course of this action, the *Saratov* Regiment fired an incredible 800,000 rounds of small-arms ammunition and its supporting artillery group fired over 10,000 rounds of 76.2mm ammunition; as the French Général Philippe Pétain would quip two years later, 'Firepower kills.'

As the attempted German right hook was being repulsed, Adaridi committed his division reserve, the *Troitsky* Regiment, to defeat the German left hook being made by 87. Infanterie-Brigade. The two regiments in Hahn's brigade had been decimated by Russian artillery enfilade fire for nearly three hours and had no support of their own; taken in flank by a fresh Russian regiment they retreated in disorder, falling back 15km. Although Mackensen had sent 69. Infanterie-Brigade (36. Infanterie-Division) in a forced march to strike the right flank of 40th Infantry Division (4th Corps), the German troops did not accomplish this mission until 1500hrs, by which time XVII. Armeekorps' attack was falling apart. Adaridi was informed that his southern flank was vulnerable but made no changes to his sound dispositions.

At 1715hrs, Mackensen committed his corps reserve, the fresh Infanterie-Regiment *von Borcke* (4. Pommersches) Nr. 21, to make a third assault upon Mattischkehmen. Mackensen, mounted on his white horse, moved forward to observe the action with his staff. Although he finally managed to get his corps artillery into the fight, it was also unable to suppress the Russian defences in the town. German survivors of the earlier attacks tried to discourage the fresh regiment from going in, but it did so, with senior officers mounted on their horses. The Russian artillerymen and machine-gunners must have been amazed to see another futile effort and they waited until the German infantry reached within about 750m of the town before commencing a concentrated barrage that knocked down dozens. The rest of the German infantrymen dropped to the ground and would advance no further. As Hesse stated: 'Feeling death raging through their ranks, the men were seized with terror in the presence of the invisible enemy. They began to break, at first slowly and then more quickly … until at length panic gained the victory …' (Hesse 1922). One of Mackensen's staff officers also witnessed the consequences:

> In the early afternoon, the first signs of retreat … began to be seen. At first, we saw individuals, then small and large bodies of troops crumbling, some of them passing the location of the corps commander. Officers of the staff halted them and organized them into a firing line, facing the enemy again, even if they weren't sent back to the battle-line. (Quoted in Mackensen 1938: 40)

By 1800hrs, both German infantry divisions were in full retreat and 3rd Corps mounted a brief pursuit, hastening the Germans back to their starting positions. Adaridi's 27th Infantry Division had suffered just 971 casualties in the battle, including 249 in the *Ufimsky* Regiment. In contrast, Mackensen's XVII. Armeekorps left over 2,000 dead on the battlefield and 1,000 prisoners, with a further 5,000 wounded. Most of the losses were in 35. Infanterie-Division, which suffered particularly heavy losses of junior officers (eight officers of the rank of *Hauptmann* and 19 of the rank of *Leutnant* dead or missing). Eschewing proper reconnaissance and co-ordinated fire support, Mackensen had squandered nearly a quarter of his infantry by choosing to fight a battle employing tactics reminiscent of the mid-19th century. Russian marksmanship was apparent on the enemy corpses, many of whom had been felled by head and chest shots.

Despite François' success against a single Russian infantry division, the bloody repulse of Mackensen's entire XVII. Armeekorps marked the battle of Gumbinnen as a Russian tactical victory, which had operational-level impact. After this defeat, 8. Armee retreated westwards and Prittwitz – who was unnerved by the defeat – was relieved of command and replaced by Generaloberst Paul von Hindenburg on 23 August. However, even before Hindenburg arrived, 8. Armee was pivoting to deal with Samsonov's Second Army, which was now crossing the border in force. In just a week, Samsonov would be defeated in detail in the battle of Tannenberg and three Russian infantry corps forced to surrender. Although 8. Armee had left only a small covering force while dealing with Samsonov, Rennenkampf had not taken serious advantage of the situation and his First Army waited for two days before cautiously advancing westwards at a sluggish pace, opposed only by Landsturm rearguards. On 25 August, Yepanchin's 3rd Corps captured Insterburg after defeating the small garrison and advanced to within 35–40km of Königsberg, but this was the Russian high-water mark. Once news arrived that Samsonov had been crushed at Tannenberg, it became clear that the Russian numerical advantage – and the strategic initiative – in East Prussia had evaporated.

The German victory at Tannenberg is celebrated in this 1914 postcard. (IMAGNO/ Archiv Jontes/TopFoto)

Göritten

7 November 1914

BACKGROUND TO BATTLE

Rennenkampf immediately shifted his First Army onto the defensive and tried to establish a linear front, but there was too much terrain and not enough troops. Even with the transfer of 2nd Corps from Samsonov's Second Army and the arrival of 22nd Corps, Rennenkampf's flanks were up in the air. Emboldened by the arrival of the Garde-Reservekorps and XI. Armeekorps from the West, Hindenburg moved quickly to drive Rennenkampf's army from East Prussian soil. In order to deceive Rennenkampf, Hindenburg ordered five Landwehr regiments from Königsberg to mount a demonstration attack against Yepanchin's 3rd Corps at Klein Schönau on 1–2 September. This sector was held by Adaridi's 27th Infantry Division, which fired off 5,000 artillery rounds to keep the

Russian infantry marching. The soldier in the foreground appears to have acquired a German-style knapsack. Both sides were quick to use captured enemy kit, since their own resupply stocks were going to form new units. (Courtesy of the Central Museum of the Armed Forces, Moscow via Stavka)

Landwehr at bay – a lavish use of ammunition that Rennenkampf's army could not afford. However, the threat to Rennenkampf's army was coming not from the west, but actually from the south. Hindenburg used the railways to shift all his forces quickly from Tannenberg to mass against Rennenkampf's left flank, near the south end of the Masurian Lakes. Russian intelligence on German dispositions and movements was negligible, leaving Rennenkampf without the information needed to deploy his forces properly against the impending threat.

On 7 September, Hindenburg began attacking Rennenkampf's left flank with I. and XVII. Armeekorps and quickly achieved success; 2nd Corps put up a good fight but was eventually forced to withdraw. Although the main body of First Army, including 3rd, 4th and 20th corps, was still intact, Rennenkampf could see that the Germans were threatening to envelop his left flank and he ordered his entire army to retreat on the night of 9/10 September. On 11 September, Yepanchin's 3rd Corps evacuated Insterburg. Zhilinski sent the reserve infantry divisions forward from Grodno to assist Rennenkampf's retreat, but these newly organized units performed poorly and were brushed aside by the Germans – demonstrating the distinct difference in quality between Russian regular and reserve infantry units. By 14 September, it was clear that Hindenburg had won another major tactical victory in the first battle of the Masurian Lakes – but the victory was primarily over Rennenkampf's second-line units. Russian infantry losses could be replaced, but a great deal of artillery and ammunition was lost in the retreat. Zhilinski, who had proved completely ineffectual as a front commander, was sacked on 17 September, but Rennenkampf, thanks to his connections in the Tsar's court, managed to keep his command for another two months. General ot infanterii Nikolai Ruzsky (1854–1918), who had ably proved himself in Galicia, took over command of the Russian North-Western Front.

After the ejection of First Army from East Prussia, the German strategic focus shifted southwards towards the Russian forces around Warsaw and the

German infantry deployed in shallow trenches at Lötzen. Note the iron crosses on their helmet covers instead of regimental numbers; these men are a mix of Reservists and Landwehr. 8. Armee had low regard for defensive tactics and usually assigned static-defence missions on the Angerapp-Stellung to second- or third-rate units. (Author)

front line east of the Masurian Lakes became stalemated. Due to the threat of a Russian advance into Silesia from Poland, Hindenburg was able to convince the OHL (Oberste Heeresleitung, the German Supreme Command) to form a second German army on the Eastern Front, 9. Armee at Breslau (now Wrocław, Poland), of which he took personal command. In order to create this new formation, Hindenburg stripped 8. Armee of XVII. and XX. Armeekorps and used these forces to mount a bold offensive towards Warsaw on 9 October, which was repulsed by a resurgent Russian Second Army; the Germans suffered over 21,000 casualties for no gain.

François, left in command of a much-weakened 8. Armee with I. Armeekorps, I. Reservekorps and Landwehr units, was instructed merely to keep the Russians out of East Prussia. Rennenkampf's troops got their first respite since the beginning of the war and they used this time to reorganize and absorb replacements from Russia's interior military districts. By mid-October 1914, Rennenkampf's first-line infantry corps had been partly restored to fighting trim and the original units in his army were absorbed into the new Tenth Army under General ot infanterii Baron Thaddeus von Sievers, a 61-year-old noble of Baltic-German heritage. Like many Russian senior commanders, Sievers was more of an administrator than a combat leader and his knowledge of modern warfare was very limited. Artillery ammunition was now in short supply in the Russian Army due to failures to predict combat expenditure accurately, and the lavish expenditure of rounds that had characterized Russian attacks in August was now prohibited.

I. Reservekorps, under the capable leadership of General der Infanterie Otto von Below, had crossed into Lithuania and occupied several towns, including Verzhbolovo on the main east–west railway line. Below's intent was to create an outer defensive perimeter beyond the East Prussian border to deter Russian cavalry raids. However, the affect was counter-productive because Sievers was soon under pressure from Stavka (the Russian High Command) to push these Germans out of Lithuania. Stavka was also eager to avenge Tannenberg by mounting another effort into East Prussia in order to divert German forces from the main battle developing in western Poland around Lodz.

On 29 October, Adaridi's 27th Infantry Division was assembled near Noviniki, 2km east of the Prussian border. One of Below's infantry regiments had occupied the village of Kopsodze south of Verzhbolovo and fortified it. Unwilling to mount a frontal assault against fortified villages without adequate artillery support, Adaridi decided to mount an unusual night attack against Kopsodze at 0300hrs on 31 October with the 106th, 107th and 108th Infantry regiments. Adaridi planned for the three regiments to converge on the village, with Polkovnik Orlovsky's 107th Infantry Regiment *Troitsky* approaching in column through a swampy area on the eastern side of the village that was believed to be unguarded. The 106th Infantry Regiment *Ufimsky* would attack from the north-east and the 108th Infantry Regiment *Saratov* from the south-east. However, the German Reservists defending the village detected the impending attack and brought artillery fire upon Orlovsky's column while it was still crossing the swamp, inflicting 76 casualties, including a battalion commander. Without the help of the flank attack from Orlovsky's *Troitsky* Regiment, the other two Russian regiments advanced in silence to mount frontal attacks against an alerted defence.

German troops posing with a captured Russian border sign, autumn 1914. These appear to be older troops, probably from a Reserve regiment. (Author)

German machine guns and field guns ripped into the advancing infantry, while German infantrymen fired back from trenches dug inside the village. Kapitan Andrei A. Uspenskiy, serving with the *Ufimsky* Regiment, recalled:

> But here, and we began the ascent up from the river and immediately [we came under fire] and there were killed and wounded ... Screams and moans from the seriously wounded sharply violated the discipline of the silent attack ... The Germans took us in a crossfire: their guns were arranged in a horseshoe ... Our attack finally stopped! ... And it seemed that our goal – their trenches – was so close! We could clearly hear their voices ...

Some Russian infantry under Leytenant Nikolai N. Nechayev managed to fight their way into the village and captured a building, despite the German firepower advantage. A night action is very confusing and the Germans were probably not sure how many Russians had actually entered the village. Nevertheless, Nechayev's men were too few to overwhelm the defence and these bold troops were either eliminated or forced to retreat before dawn. The *Ufimsky* Regiment suffered 91 casualties and, altogether, Adaridi had lost over 300 men, including a number of officers. German losses were only about one-third of the Russian losses, but it was now apparent that Below's I. Reservekorps was holding too many exposed positions and on 6 November the Germans decided to withdraw westwards towards Stallupönen. 1. Reserve-Division abandoned its strongly fortified position in the town of Verzhbolovo inside Lithuania and retired to prepared positions at Stallupönen. The weather was also beginning to change, with colder temperatures and night frost beginning to affect troops deployed in field positions. The cold did not bother the Russians much, but the German troops preferred to be on friendly soil as the weather worsened.

MAP KEY

1 Early morning: The 106th Infantry Regiment *Ufimsky* seizes the undefended village of Göritten.

2 Mid-morning: 1. Reserve-Division, supported by Landwehr, strikes the flank of the 105th Infantry Regiment *Orenburg* and forces it to pull back. German infantrymen fight their way into Göritten.

3 Late morning: The Russian reserve, two battalions of the 107th Infantry Regiment *Troitsky*, counter-attacks and regains a foothold in Göritten. The *Orenburg* and *Ufimsky* regiments re-form.

4 1330–1400hrs: The Germans renew their assault on 27th Infantry Division's right flank, pounding the *Orenburg*

Regiment, which mounts a desperate bayonet attack and stabilizes the front.

5 Afternoon: 72. Reserve-Infanterie-Brigade is committed to try to outflank the Russian positions around Göritten.

6 Afternoon: The 108th Infantry Regiment *Saratov* is committed to stabilize the Russian left flank.

7 1700hrs: The Germans renew their attack on the right flank and overrun the *Orenburg* Regiment. Two Russian artillery batteries are nearly overrun.

8 After 1700hrs: 27th Infantry Division is ordered to retreat, even though the Germans are exhausted.

Battlefield environment

Saturday 7 November 1914 was an overcast day, with low, brooding clouds that offered the possibility of a late-morning shower. There was some haze, which would aid the attacking Germans. The morning temperature was just above freezing, 0–3 degrees Celsius. By noon, it would rise to about 5 degrees; this chill would make it difficult for soldiers to operate their bolt-action rifles quickly, with fingers stiff and awkward. The wind was from the south-south-west, into the Russians' faces.

Göritten was a crossroads settlement, bisected both by an east–west dirt road and by a north–south road leading to Stallupönen. It was a good-sized village, with a few large agricultural storage warehouses, a stout brick church and a *Gästehaus*, in addition to about 30 houses. There were also a couple of tall grain silos which offered vantage as observation posts.

Göritten was bounded to the north and east by two streams, which impeded dismounted movement in or out of the village. On the western side of Göritten, trees and underbrush obstructed direct observation into the village. By early November, Göritten had suffered considerable damage from both armies moving through the area and some buildings had been fired or broken up for firewood. There were some infantry positions dug around the village's perimeter, but not yet true trench works. The area surrounding Göritten is mostly flat farmland, particularly to the west of the village. By early November, the fields were barren and muddy. It had rained off and on for a week or so, leaving the low-lying ground water-logged. There were small clumps of wooded areas, with thick underbrush, that offered some cover and the ground sloped downwards towards Stallupönen.

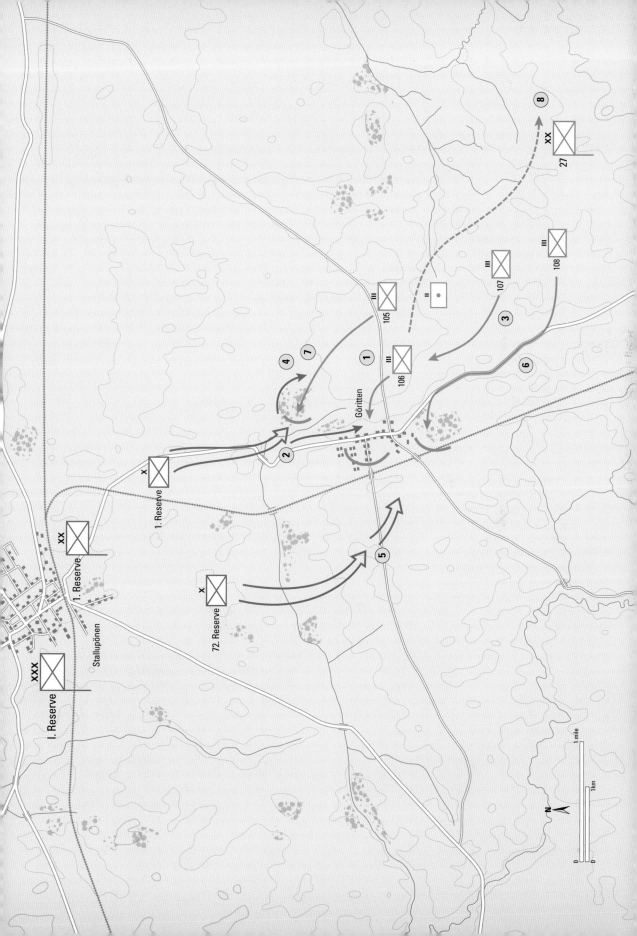

I. Reserve

XXX

Stallupönen

XX
1. Reserve

X
1. Reserve

X
72. Reserve

2

5

4
7

Göritten

1
III
106

105
III

II

107
III

3

108
III

6

105
III

XX
27

8

N

0   1km
0   1 mile

INTO COMBAT

Russian skirmishers in an East Prussian village, probably around the time of the battle of Göritten in November 1914. Note that there is already one casualty on the ground, so the enemy is likely in contact. Russian techniques in battlefield medicine were quite advanced since Dr Nikolai Pirogov had pioneered field surgery and the triage concept 60 years earlier, during the Crimean War (1853–56). However, Russian medical capabilities were undermined by inefficient transport services, which often proved unable to move wounded troops back to railheads in a timely manner; often, wounded Russian personnel remained near the battlefield for days or weeks until they could be transported. (Scherl / SZ Photo)

Sievers ordered Yepanchin's 3rd Corps to mount a pursuit across the border and occupy Stallupönen and vicinity – a rather tall order for a single corps. In the early-morning hours of 7 November, Adaridi's 27th Infantry Division advanced with its 105th Infantry Regiment *Orenburg* and the *Ufimsky* Regiment, with the other two regiments in support. Even after three months of combat, Polkovnik Otryganev's *Ufimsky* Regiment still had 3,000 troops, but the *Orenburg* Regiment was reduced to a 500-man battle group. As they crossed the border, the troops of the *Ufimsky* Regiment came under long-range artillery fire and glimpsed some German cavalry patrols, but encountered no formed enemy resistance. Otryganev reported that the Germans appeared to be a rearguard and managed to capture the unoccupied village of Göritten, 4km south of Stallupönen. Otryganev immediately set about establishing a defence, while waiting for the rest of the division to come up. Only two 76.2mm field-artillery batteries reached the village to support his defence.

In fact, the Germans were not a rearguard and this became apparent when the lead elements of 1. Reserve-Division and Landwehr-Division *Königsberg* appeared from the north-west, marching fast from Stallupönen. By evacuating their forward positions along the border, the units of I. Reservekorps had regained a suitable mass for the preferred German tactic: a well-timed counter-attack. The German Reservists came on quickly in column, with little artillery or machine-gun support, but they struck the flank of 27th Infantry Division before it had entrenched or tied in with its lagging neighbour, 25th Infantry Division. Apparently, Russian scouts failed to report the approaching German columns or wrongly interpreted them to be retreating units; either way, it was a meeting engagement in which only one side was aware of the other.

Once again, the hapless *Orenburg* Regiment was guarding the exposed Russian right flank and it was overwhelmed in a sea of *Feldgrau*, despite a futile stand. After the *Orenburg* Regiment was overrun, 1. Reserve-Division took Otryganev's *Ufimsky* Regiment in the flank and boldly pushed a brigade into Göritten, which was not yet fortified. Just as the Germans seemed on the cusp of a clear tactical victory, however, the Russian infantrymen dug in their heels. Adaridi quickly committed his reserve – two battalions of the *Troitsky* Regiment – which regained part of the village in a bayonet attack and caused the Germans to pause. German infantry, particularly older Reservists, had little taste for costly close-quarters combat and instead played by the book, waiting for their artillery and machine-gun detachments to deploy and force the remaining Russians to withdraw. Once the Russians recovered from the shock of the sudden German counter-attack, the innate tenacity of the Russian infantrymen allowed a hasty defence to be cobbled together. During World War I, Russian infantrymen displayed a great talent for house-to-house fighting; this would reappear in World War II, as well.

After re-organizing and deploying their fire-support assets, at about 1330hrs the German Reservists mounted another attack against the remnants of the *Orenburg* Regiment on 27th Infantry Division's right flank. Amazingly, the badly depleted *Orenburg* Regiment stopped the assault, with the assistance of the field guns from Folimonov's 27th Artillery Brigade. Russian artillerymen poured shrapnel fire into the German assault columns, which was a nasty surprise for the attackers.

Faced with stiffening Russian resistance, Below attempted to outflank the Russian position at Göritten, but Adaridi committed his *Saratov* Regiment to block this effort. Adaridi might have been able to hold if he had received assistance from the rest of 3rd Corps, but Yepanchin was unaware that he was involved in a fight with elements of three German divisions, so no help arrived. Adaridi was forced to extend his division's front across 10km to prevent being outflanked by a superior force, which meant that his lines were increasingly thin. Below was able to bring up his fresh 36. Reserve-Division and at about 1700hrs, the Germans made another brigade-sized push against

Reservists comprised a large proportion of the German infantry units that fought in the early battles in East Prussia. Here, German Reservists put on their equipment during the mobilization phase in the first days of August 1914. German infantry equipment was fairly complicated for novices. Russian recruits did not require assistance in donning their much simpler kit. (Author)

Adaridi's right flank. This time, the *Orenburg* Regiment – which had suffered 75 per cent casualties – buckled and retreated. Although the German infantrymen were exhausted after the tough, close-quarter fight and in no mood for a pursuit, Yepanchin believed that Adaridi's division had collapsed and ordered it to retreat immediately. Adaridi obeyed, abandoning his remaining positions around Göritten and falling back across the border, but he was soon made the scapegoat for the defeat and relieved of command (he was later exonerated, but retired).

Adaridi's infantrymen had fought bravely at Göritten, but they had fought with virtually no support against a numerically far superior enemy force for about eight hours. The *Orenburg* Regiment suffered over 350 casualties and the *Ufimsky* Regiment, 878 losses. Overall, the Russians suffered about 1,400 casualties at Göritten and the Germans about 500. The performance of the Russian infantry at Göritten demonstrated the innate combat steadiness of Russia's first-line regiments, even when faced with horrific losses, but this could not compensate for the inability of Russian corps and army commanders to orchestrate timely supporting efforts by the rest of their forces.

The Tsar presents decorations to soldiers of his Imperial Guard on 30 December 1914. (From the fonds of the RGAKFD in Krasnogorsk via Stavka)

Mahartse

---

16 February 1915

BACKGROUND TO BATTLE

Despite Below's tactical victory against a single outnumbered Russian division at Göritten, the German attention in the East remained focused on defeating the Russian armies in Poland. Hindenburg attempted another overly bold advance towards Warsaw with 9. Armee, but his offensive was stymied at the battle of Lodz (11–26 November), where the revitalized Second Army parried the German assaults and nearly encircled a German corps. Although German propaganda depicted the Eastern Front battles of October–November 1914 as successes, in fact Hindenburg's offensives had achieved very little. The only consolation for the Germans was that the Russian Army had used up much of its artillery ammunition stocks and was forced to abandon Lodz in order to shorten the front line in Poland.

Owing to heavy losses suffered by 9. Armee in Poland, even Below's I. Reservekorps was shifted south and for a time, the only German forces left on the Insterburg front were Landwehr brigades and some cavalry. Consequently, the Germans were obliged to abandon Stallupönen and pull back away from the border. Once the Russians realized that the German strength in the area was much reduced, Sievers crossed the border and Yepanchin's 3rd Corps re-occupied Göritten on 13 November. Despite the imposing Russian superiority in this sector, Stavka was only concerned with the battle of Lodz and could not spare the resources to sustain a major advance into East Prussia. Instead, Sievers contented himself with small-scale skirmishing near Stallupönen, with his infantry units clashing with local Landwehr. Nothing much was accomplished and a virtual lull settled over the East Prussian border region during December 1914. However once the battle of Lodz ended, Stavka belatedly authorized Sievers' Tenth Army to begin advancing westwards again in January 1915. In order to spearhead the new offensive, the veteran first-line infantry divisions from 3rd Corps were transferred to 20th Corps, while Yepanchin's corps received reserve infantry divisions and cavalry to guard the army's extended right flank. By 1 February, 20th Corps was near Gumbinnen. Some Russian patrols pushed around and past the German fortified towns, which caused considerable consternation in the OHL.

The OHL had already dispatched a third corps from the Western Front to the Eastern Front at the end of 1914 and the renewed Russian incursion into East Prussia convinced the OHL to send XXI. Armeekorps, as well. Additionally, two new formations – XXXVIII. and XXXIX. Reservekorps – were raised in December 1914 and, together with XXI. Armeekorps, formed into 10. Armee under Generaloberst Hermann von Eichhorn in late January 1915 – a fact which Russian intelligence missed. Eichhorn was tasked with repulsing the Russian Tenth Army's incursion into East Prussia, with help from 8. Armee. It was highly unusual for the Germans to mount a major winter offensive on the Eastern Front and many of their troops would be third-string reservists who had missed the earlier battles. The two new *Reservekorps* had 25 per cent less infantry than the Stehendes Heer corps and far fewer machine guns and artillery pieces, but Siever's Tenth Army staff were unaware of the arrival of German reinforcements and still focused on 8. Armee to the south of the Masurian Lakes. Tenth Army was over-extended, low on supplies and not expecting a major German winter counter-offensive. In particular, the Russian Army was beginning to run very low on rifle and artillery ammunition, which seriously reduced the firepower of its infantry units.

On 7 February 1915, Eichhorn began the offensive that would be known as the second battle of the Masurian Lakes with his three corps attacking Tenth Army's right flank, held by Yepanchin's 3rd Corps. The Germans attacked during a major snowstorm and enjoyed a large numerical superiority. Yepanchin's reservists, augmented by two cavalry divisions, were outnumbered and outclassed. After a brief battle north of Stallupönen, Yepanchin's 3rd Corps disintegrated and began a precipitous retreat. Thousands of prisoners were taken and much equipment abandoned. Yepanchin failed to conduct a rearguard and instead sped to the rear, with his staff. In Grodno, Sievers was unaware of the situation for several days and failed to react.

Eichhorn's 10. Armee ploughed through the remnants of Yepanchin's routed corps and undertook a forced march 40km towards the south-east, enveloping Tenth Army's right flank. Eichhorn used his best troops from General der Infanterie Fritz von Below's XXI. Armeekorps to lead the advance while his Reservists mopped up the Russian fragments. Generalleutnant Hasso von Bredow's 42. Infanterie-Division was in the lead, with its 65. Infanterie-Brigade acting as vanguard. In a matter of days, the Germans had severed the Russian direct line of communications to Kovno. Sievers relieved Yepanchin of command but did not comprehend the scale of the defeat or the unfolding German scheme of manoeuvre, which gave Eichhorn two valuable days to manoeuvre without serious interference. Instead, Sievers was more concerned about his left flank, where 3rd Siberian Infantry Corps was hard-pressed to hold off 8. Armee's attacks south of the Masurian Lakes. By the time that Sievers realized what was going on the damage was done and he ordered his entire army to retreat towards Augustovo on 9 February. However, the front commander, General Ruzsky, rescinded the retreat order and unrealistically instructed the rest of Sievers' army to remain in place until he could organize a counter-offensive with Twelfth Army in Poland. As often happens in a catastrophe, the units at greatest risk were bombarded with orders, counter-orders and then silence.

In the centre of Tenth Army's line near Gumbinnen, General ot artillerii Pavel I. Bulgakov's 20th Corps did not receive Sievers' order to retreat or Ruzsky's counter-order, so he maintained his positions for another 24 hours. Bulgakov was an experienced commander, having led 25th Infantry Division during the battle of Gumbinnen. By the time that he realized that the Russian units on his northern flank had evaporated, XXI. Armeekorps had already force-marched units around behind his positions, trying to cut off his line of retreat. 26th Corps to his south was in a similar predicament, particularly when 3rd Siberian Infantry Corps retreated and allowed German units from 8. Armee to advance from the south. Both Russian corps in the centre were in danger of encirclement. The German infantry undertook forced marches eastwards, but quickly became strung out in columns along the forest roads. By 14 February, Bredow's 42. Infanterie-Division had reached Sejny, east of Suvalki. Yet the German advance had not gone unscathed – bitter winter temperatures exacted their own price upon the poorly clad Germans, who suffered about 4,000 frostbite casualties in a week.

Bulgakov's corps consisted of 27th, 29th and 53rd Infantry divisions. On the evening of 10 February, 20th Corps belatedly began its retreat towards Augustovo, along with elements of 26th Corps. The weather was vile, with 1m-deep snow and frigid temperatures, and the roads were unable to support heavy traffic. Even with their thick overcoats, felt boots and *ushanka* felt caps, the Russian infantrymen were also vulnerable to frostbite and the horses pulling their artillery and supply wagons were in worse shape. A winter retreat is tough on any army, even a Russian army. Nevertheless, the Russian infantrymen marched resolutely eastwards. A strong rearguard was left at Suvalki, in hopes of delaying the German pursuit. For a while, it appeared that the Russian infantry units might escape the impending German trap but after four days of marching, the 20th Corps vanguard bumped into German patrols near Tobolovo. It was clear that XXI. Armeekorps had established blocking positions across 20th Corps' line of retreat. The Germans had chosen an excellent blocking position, fortifying the village of Mahartse on the northern side of Lake Serwy. The terrain was heavily forested with few roads, most of which ran through Mahartse. Bulgakov realized that the situation was desperate and that his command would be annihilated unless something was done immediately. He turned to his most reliable unit, 27th Infantry Division, and ordered it to break through the German blocking positions and open a path for the rest of the corps to escape.

Russian infantry holding an ad hoc defensive position in the winter of 1914/15. The Russian troops were generally better trained and equipped for winter warfare than the Germans, but the Russian leadership did not know how to exploit this advantage. (Courtesy of the Central Museum of the Armed Forces, Moscow via Stavka)

Infanterie-Regiment Nr. 138 and 108th Infantry Regiment *Saratov* at Mahartse, 16 February 1915

MAP KEY

1 0700hrs: Two battalions from the 108th Infantry Regiment *Saratov* and one battalion from the 106th Infantry Regiment *Ufimsky* attack 3. Unter-Elsässisches Infanterie-Regiment Nr. 138's outposts at Dalny Las and Serski Las. Three Russian batteries fire at close range to suppress the German defences.

2 *c.*0800hrs: Polkovnik Valerian E. Belolipetsky leads two battalions of the *Saratov* Regiment through the woods to approach Mahartse, which is held by the rest of the German battalion.

3 1000hrs: A German field-grade officer is captured in Dalny Las, unaware that the Russians are in the village.

4 1000hrs: The *Ufimsky* Regiment captures Serski Las but its commander is badly wounded.

5 Late morning: 1. Oberrheinisches Infanterie-Regiment Nr. 97 is sent by circuitous route to block the southern end of Lake Serwy, but does not arrive until the battle is over.

6 Early afternoon: Several Russian companies cross the frozen ice of Lake Serwy to outflank the German defences in Mahartse.

7 1500hrs: The *Saratov* Regiment continues the attack against Mahartse, which the Germans decide to abandon. The Russians capture about 1,000 prisoners and 13 guns.

8 Late afternoon: Infanterie-Regiment Nr. 138 marches with a reinforced battalion to assist the defenders in Mahartse but does not arrive until the action is nearly over. It then establishes blocking positions on the road to Frącki.

Battlefield environment

Tuesday 16 February 1915 was another overcast day, but colder, with morning temperatures hovering around freezing. Wind-chill, with a stiff breeze blowing from the south, made it feel like –4 degrees Celsius; this didn't affect the warmly clad Russians, but it made the German troops sitting in static positions miserable after a few hours. Dawn, which arrived at about 0800hrs, brought a light drizzle, which changed to light snow before noon. Visibility alternated between hazy and clear.

Mahartse and the other outlying villages of Serski Las and Dalny Las were little more than hamlets, each with a few wooden houses and barns. This area was yet to see much combat until now, so the buildings were mostly intact and provided a measure of protection against the elements for some of the troops. However, Mahartse lay at a crossroads which was vital for the Russian withdrawal route and it was necessary for them to keep a considerable security force outside to cover all approaches. Although the German positions in Mahartse had decent short-range visibility to the south-west, thick pine forests blocked visibility to the west and north.

At Dalny Las, the Germans only had visibility down the main road to a distance of 300m, which meant that Russian infantry could get well within rifle range before being spotted. The area around Serski Las was far more open, with flat farmland, and here the Germans could observe the approaches out to 500m or so. The ground was hard, which made any kind of digging difficult. Lake Serwy, which was frozen and dusted with snow, bounded the south-eastern corner of the village. It was a narrow lake, bounded by tall trees – which made it difficult to observe anyone crossing it from a distance.

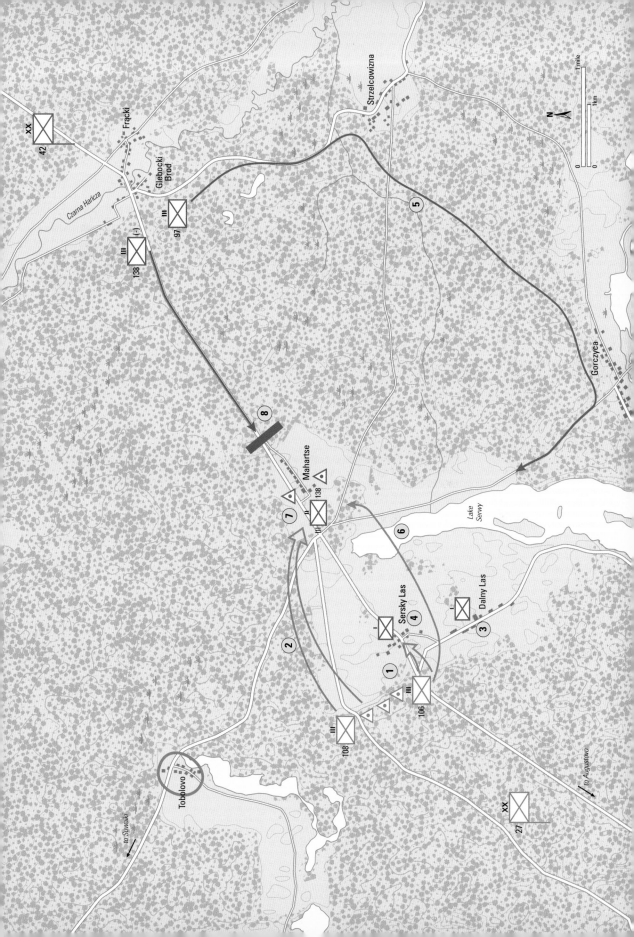

INTO COMBAT

Polkovnik Vladimir N. von Dreyer, chief of staff of 27th Infantry Division, took charge of organizing the Russian break-out effort. Dreyer was another ethnic German who had been born in Russia and drawn to military service; he was no less competent and aggressive than the Prussian officers he was opposing. After six months of active service at the front, 27th Infantry Division was in poor condition and its infantry regiments were reduced to 50 per cent or less of authorized strength. Only Polkovnik Valerian E. Belolipetsky's 108th Infantry Regiment *Saratov* was still capable of fielding four understrength battalions, whereas Polkovnik Otryganev's 106th Infantry Regiment *Ufimsky* was reduced to only a single battalion and the remnants of the 105th Infantry Regiment *Orenburg* were barely equal to a company. At best, 27th Infantry Division could employ five battalion equivalents at Mahartse, down from the 16 battalions that it had started with in August 1914. Nor had the winter retreat helped the division's condition, requiring considerable material to be abandoned and leaving the survivors short of ammunition and rations. Nevertheless, Dreyer cobbled together an assault force on the night of 15/16 February; he selected Polkovnik Belolipetsky to lead the main body and provided him with the last three operational artillery batteries. Although Bulgakov promised assistance from other units in 20th Corps, the only reinforcement to materialize was a company-sized force from the 334th Infantry Regiment.

The Russians were not sure of the size of the German force blocking their escape, but believed it to be the bulk of Generalleutnant Hasso von Bredow's 42. Infanterie-Division from XXI. Armeekorps. In fact, Bredow had only managed to get a single *Vorausabteilung* (advance battalion) from his division to Mahartse before the Russians, and the rest of his 42. Infanterie-Division was still en route. III. Bataillon/3. Unter-Elsässisches Infanterie-Regiment Nr. 138 occupied Mahartse on 15 February and established company-sized outposts at Serski Las and Dalny Las, but the rest of the regiment was still 5km or more to the north-east. The other regiment in 59. Infanterie-Brigade, 1. Oberrheinisches Infanterie-Regiment Nr. 97, was also approaching but Bredow ordered it to proceed by a circuitous route to the southern end of Lake Serwy, so it would play no role in the coming battle. The Germans had managed to get two artillery batteries to Mahartse, but did not have time to dig in or construct obstacles. Consequently, when the Russian attack commenced at 0700hrs on 16 February, there were about five Russian infantry battalions opposing a single German infantry battalion. Bredow, well to the rear, was unaware of the Russian dispositions or the threat to his advance guard.

Belolipetsky expected heavy resistance around Mahartse and in order to gain fire superiority early in the action, he decided to adopt a novel tactic. He brought all three artillery batteries up on line with his infantry skirmishers, who were deployed at the edge of the dense Augustovo Forest. The two German-held villages were barely 400m away and the Russian gun crews were well within range of enemy marksmen. However, Belolipetsky's gamble paid off thanks to the presence of early-morning mist and the Russian gunners were able to deploy their 76.2mm field guns and get into action without serious interference from the Germans. The Russian gunners began the battle by firing over open sights, pounding the villages with shrapnel and high-explosive rounds, which effectively suppressed the German outposts. As at Mattischkehmen, this kind of bombardment could not destroy the target, but it discouraged the Germans from revealing their positions by firing. Under cover of their guns, the Russian infantrymen from the *Saratov* and *Ufimsky* regiments moved out of the forests and quickly crossed the snow-covered fields, with bayonets fixed. Apparently, the Germans had not brought up their machine-gun detachments yet – they were still in Mahartse – but once they saw the enemy approaching the German infantrymen laid down rapid fire in an effort to stop the oncoming waves of Russian infantrymen.

German infantrymen with two well-dressed Russian prisoners during the winter of 1914/15. During the Russian retreat from East Prussia, thousands of troops were cut off or isolated in the forests and were scooped up by German patrols. Note that the Russian uniforms and healthy appearance of the prisoners is indicative of the pre-war Russian Army in the early stages of World War I. (Nik Cornish at www.stavka.org.uk)

Polkovnik Konstantin P. Otryganev led his composite battalion from the *Ufimsky* Regiment forward into a hail of German rifle fire coming from Serski Las. After advancing some distance, Otryganev was struck in the leg by a rifle bullet and unable to continue, so he handed over command to another officer. While the German fire was heavy, they were badly outnumbered here and rifle fire alone could not counter these odds. Soon, the Russian infantrymen stormed into the village and the Germans retreated into peasant *izba* (huts), causing the action to degenerate into a close-quarters house-to-house fight. Yet the Russians had the upper hand and the *Ufimsky* Regiment succeeded in clearing both Serski Las and Dalny Las by 1000hrs. The two German infantry companies in the village outposts were badly mauled, with 39 dead in 10. Kompanie and 43 dead in 11. Kompanie. The survivors fled towards Mahartse. During the action, a German *Oberst* from 42. Infanterie-Division drove into Dalny Las in his staff car, unaware that Russian troops were in the village – and was promptly captured. German tactical-level command and control during the battle of Mahartse was remarkably poor, which greatly levelled the playing field.

Meanwhile, Belolipetsky had bypassed the two German strongpoints with two battalions from his *Saratov* Regiment and advanced through the edge of woods directly towards Mahartse, where the rest of the German infantry battalion was located. Initially, the Germans in Mahartse were able to slow down Belolipetsky's infantrymen, with the assistance of two 7.7cm batteries and some machine guns, but the situation changed once the two outposts were lost. A Russian company commander from the *Saratov* Regiment's reserve battalion, Shtabs-Kapitan Melenevskii, organized a force of perhaps 120 infantrymen and marched across the ice of Lake Serwy in order to attack Mahartse from the south. No German units were covering the frozen lake since it did not seem a likely avenue of approach and initially, the Germans were unaware of this over-ice attack because of the presence of dense trees around the lake. However, once Russian infantry began to appear behind the

Assaulting Mahartse

After overrunning the German company-sized outposts in the villages of Serski Las and Dalny Las, two battalions from the Russian 108th Infantry Regiment *Saratov* tried to capture the town of Mahartse, which was held by the remainder of III. Bataillon/Infanterie-Regiment Nr. 138. The Germans had sufficient firepower to stop the Russian main attack, but their flanks were vulnerable. Seeing the main attack stymied, Shtabs-Kapitan Melenevskii, a company commander from the *Saratov* Regiment's reserve battalion, pulled together a composite assault group and led them across the ice of frozen

Lake Serwy to outflank Mahartse from the south. The Germans were not expecting an over-ice attack – this was definitely not in their 1906 regulations – and this lack of imagination compromised their defence. Melenevskii's infantrymen were able to cross the ice and reach the edge of the town before the Germans noticed them and this surprise caused the Germans to abandon the town. Here, the Russian infantry are advancing across the ice with bayonets fixed, while a few rounds of Russian artillery fire land in the town and a firefight is occurring on the far side of town.

town, the remainder of the personnel of III. Bataillon/Infanterie-Regiment Nr. 138 realized that they had been outflanked and opted to withdraw from Mahartse and fall back towards the division's main body in Frącki. By 1500hrs, the *Saratov* Regiment had taken Mahartse. III. Bataillon/Infanterie-Regiment Nr. 138 suffered 107 dead, including three officers and 13 NCOs. The Russians captured 13 field guns in Mahartse – which the Germans had abandoned – and claimed to have taken about 1,000 prisoners. Bredow had sent the rest of Infanterie-Regiment Nr. 138 down the road from Frącki to support the defence of Mahartse, but by the time it arrived the town was already being evacuated. Lacking artillery support, the German regiment instead established blocking positions and awaited reinforcements. Infanterie-Regiment Nr. 97 was diverted from the southern side of Lake Serwy in order to reinforce the depleted Infanterie-Regiment Nr. 138, which gave Bredow about five battalions to block the northern end of the lake.

After taking Mahartse, the remnants of 27th Infantry Division were ordered to hold a route to the east open for the rest of 20th and 26th corps to escape the pocket. Marching south of Lake Serwy, 26th Corps succeeded in escaping because Infanterie-Regiment Nr. 97 had been diverted to deal with the Russian counter-attack at Mahartse. A lone German battalion from Bredow's 42. Infanterie-Division, I. Bataillon/Infanterie-Regiment *Graf Barfuß* (4.Westfälisches) Nr. 17, managed to intercept, but quickly found itself surrounded at Sajenek, east of Augustovo. This isolated German battalion was annihilated by the escaping 26th Corps. Yet despite this minor tactical victory, Bulgakov's 20th Corps soon discovered that five German infantry battalions with artillery support were now blocking their intended route north of the lake. Indeed, Bulgakov's 20th Corps had not escaped the German encirclement, and now its strength and ammunition were nearly spent. XXI. Armeekorps closed in, establishing a tighter cordon around Bulgakov's corps, the elements of which retreated into the forests in order to conceal their positions from German artillery. In desperation, on 19 March Belolipetsky asked for volunteers to try to slip through the German lines in order to reach Sievers' headquarters in Grodno and obtain help from the rest of Tenth Army. Amazingly, a 12-year-old local boy who knew the forest was able to slip through the German cordon and deliver a message, but Sievers believed that 20th Corps had already surrendered and that this was some kind of trick. No help was sent.

Abandoned, the remnants of Bulgakov's 20th Corps huddled in the snow-covered Augustovo Forest, without rations, and waited for the end. A large number of German prisoners were still in custody and the Russians made every effort to protect them – a stark contrast to how both sides treated prisoners on the Eastern Front in 1941–45. By 21 February, the Russian infantrymen were running out of ammunition and the defence began to collapse. Many troops, led by an officer or NCO, attempted to escape through the forest towards Russian lines. Polkovnik Belolipetsky managed to escape the pocket with part of his *Saratov* Regiment, and Polkovnik Vladimir N. von Dreyer, the 27th Infantry Division chief of staff, also escaped. Yet for many of the pre-war Russian regulars who had crossed into East Prussia in August 1914, this was the end of the road. Over 12,000 Russian troops were captured in the Augustovo Forest, including General Bulgakov and his entire corps staff. 27. Infantry Division was virtually annihilated; General-mayor Folimonov, commander of 27th Artillery Brigade, and General-mayor Beymelburg were both captured. Polkovnik Konstantin Otryganev was captured along with the remnants of his *Ufimsky* Regiment and he died of his wounds in captivity.

By the beginning of 1915 the war along the East Prussian border had assumed a static character and the Russians began to construct trenches. The Russian infantry were well provided with warm winter uniforms, although they were beginning to run short on ammunition. (Courtesy of the Central Museum of the Armed Forces, Moscow via Stavka)

Altogether, the German winter counter-offensive in the second battle of the Masurian Lakes had captured or killed over 100,000 soldiers from Tenth Army in a matter of two weeks, and even the Russian units that had escaped the trap were decimated. After these defeats on the borders of East Prussia, the Russian North-Western Front would be comprised mostly of second- and third-rate reserve units that were incapable of the kind of combat performance achieved by the old pre-war regiments. Consequently, the initiative in this sector passed irretrievably to the Germans, although 10. Armee lacked the strength or logistical support to exploit its victory immediately and make any major push eastwards. Instead, the Germans shifted their attention to eliminating the Russian forces in Poland and the front in Lithuania entered a temporary static phase.

Analysis

Examination of the three actions fought at Gumbinnen, Göritten and Mahartse allows us to assess the combat performance of 27th Infantry Division's regular Russian infantry regiments and their German opponents during the opening phase of World War I. Unlike later actions, the Russian units in these actions still consisted primarily of pre-war regulars and were not seriously degraded by morale issues and ammunition shortages were not yet crippling. The opposing German infantry regiments were a mix of Stehendes Heer and Reserve units. In the battle of Gumbinnen, 27th Infantry Division conducted a successful hasty defence against XVII. Armeekorps. At Göritten, 27th Infantry Division was involved in a meeting engagement against I. Reservekorps and came off the worse. At Mahartse, the remnants of 27th Infantry Division conducted a successful hasty attack against a reinforced German infantry battalion from 42. Infanterie-Division, although the Russians failed to achieve an operational-level break-out. These three actions are illustrative of the opposing doctrines and tactics in both offensive and defensive conditions, as well as in summer and winter settings.

Although the theoretical German superiority in heavy artillery is often claimed to be a decisive factor, the Russian First Army enjoyed considerable artillery support in the early stages of the invasion of East Prussia. Here, a battery of 122mm M1909 howitzers prepares to fire. (Author)

A German MG 08 machine gun in prone firing position. While the MG 08 had a lower rate of fire than the Russian Maxim machine gun, the MG 08 had a significantly better muzzle velocity, which increased the penetration of its rounds. However, the MG 08 was an awkward weapon which was extremely heavy and difficult to get into action quickly in a fast-moving engagement and it required frequent barrel changes when firing. Nor did the MG 08 have a gun shield like the Russian Maxim to protect the gunner; it would not receive one until April 1915. Overall, the MG 08 performed best as a defensive weapon, but was difficult to employ as an infantry-support weapon in the attack. (Author)

MOBILITY, FIREPOWER AND THE DEFENCE

Both sides' regular infantry regiments were quite good at forced marches, in summer or winter, but it was the Germans who proved particularly adept at manoeuvring to an exposed flank. Russian battalion-level counter-attacks were often well executed and ably led by their officers. Russian combat experience from the Russo-Japanese War was a bit of an advantage at the outset, particularly in instilling a greater respect for firepower and the value of digging in on a captured objective as quickly as possible. Russian artillery support and use of machine guns was probably superior to the German performance in these early actions, but once the Russians began to lose their artillery and machine guns in the retreats of 1915, their infantry units became far more fragile. The Russians were every bit as likely as the Germans to attempt repeated frontal attacks on prepared positions, however. Karl von Wiegand, a German-born US war correspondent, recounted his impression of the Russians' third attempt to storm German positions at Wirballen (now Virbalis in Lithuania) on 8 October 1914:

> At a number of points along their line, observable by us, but screened from the observation of the German trenches in the centre, the Russian infantry came tumbling out, and, rushing forward, took up advanced positions, awaiting the formation of the new and irregular battle line. Dozens of light rapid-firers [presumably Maxim guns] were dragged along by hand. Other troops – the reserves – took up semi-advanced positions. All the while the Russian shrapnel was raining over the German trenches.
>
> Finally came the Russian order to advance. At the word, hundreds of yards of the Russian fighting line leaped forward, deployed in open order and came on. One, two, three, and in some places four and five successive skirmish lines, separated by intervals of 20 to 50 yards [18–46m], swept forward. Some of them came into range of the German trench fire almost at once. These lines began to wilt and thin out. Others were able to make a considerable advance under cover …
>
> … And then came a new sight. A few seconds later came a new sound. First I saw a sudden, almost grotesque, melting of the advancing lines … The men

literally went down like dominoes in a row. Those who kept their feet were hurled back as though by a terrible gust of wind. Almost in the second that I pondered, the staccato rattle of machine-guns reached us. My ear answered the query of my eye. (Quoted in Russell 1919: 212–13)

Generalleutnant Curt von Morgen, commander of 3. Reserve-Division and then I. Reserve-Korps in 1914–15, offered some useful points about the Russian infantry in a post-war book notable for its strong anti-Russian bias:

The Russian infantry has a great capacity for marching. Frequently, prisoner interrogation revealed they had covered 60km a day on poor roads and with poor supplies. However, the Russian infantryman is less encumbered than the German. Like their capacity for marching, the readiness of the Russian infantry to establish field positions must be acknowledged. They are masters of the subject. (Morgen 1920: 56–57)

It is noticeable that entrenchments were really only a factor at Gumbinnen and that these infantry actions were not fought under the kind of trench-warfare conditions that had appeared on the Western Front in the autumn of 1914. Yet it is clear that the Russian infantry were quite adept at defensive combat and that the German infantry could only defeat regular Russian infantry by means of cleverly executed flank attacks. At no point do we see German infantry gain fire superiority over Russian infantry, as German pre-war doctrine dictated. Nor was Russian artillery seriously outgunned in any of these early actions. Indeed, Russian tactical-level firepower was more than adequate in these opening actions, if somewhat dependent upon extravagant expenditures of ammunition.

Although it is true that the German infantry divisions and corps had more organic artillery support than their Russian counterparts, the German superiority in artillery did not actually affect the tactical outcome in any of the early actions against the Russian First or Tenth armies. The role of heavy artillery would not become significant until the war on the Eastern Front assumed a more positional character in early 1915, but in the initial mobile battles it had not been a decisive factor. German 15cm howitzers were slow to get into action at Gumbinnen and they failed to pulverize the Russian defenders in Mattischkehmen. Most of the early Eastern Front battles were essentially meeting engagements and usually only small numbers of artillery batteries were brought into action before a decision was reached.

MORALE AND REPLACEMENTS

One senior Russian officer who fought in 1914–15, General ot Kavallerii Vasily Gurko, was struck by the Germans' approach to different types of engagement:

[The Germans] showed a certain impetuousity, and one could notice the personal initiative, not only of the smaller units, but even of small bodies of infantry, even when they were without officers. On the other hand, in defensive open fighting they did not distinguish themselves by any extraordinary tenacity of purpose, and when they began to retire after a battle their power of resistance dwindled to vanishing point. (Gurko 1919: 40)

As casualties mounted, the pre-war regulars and trained reservists who fought the battles of 1914 were augmented by troops raised in wartime. Mackensen noted the effect of large numbers of untried, hastily trained troops reinforcing depleted units at the front after November 1914:

My troops have just had their first replacements sent to them and are once more at full fighting strength. But there are many wartime volunteers amongst them, with barely five weeks' training behind them. I would have wished for these young people to undergo longer training. Courage and enthusiasm alone are not sufficient. Tight discipline, fitness and marksmanship can't be learned quickly, and they form the basis for the wartime skills of the infantry. (Mackensen 1938: 65)

COMMAND AND CONTROL

Although the Germans are generally believed to have had better command and control, particularly at the operational levels, it was not always true at the tactical level. At Gumbinnen, Mackensen sent his infantrymen against an alert and prepared Russian defence that shredded his assault regiments. At Mahartse, Bredow was ignorant of Russian dispositions and failed to deploy his division in a timely manner to defeat the Russian break-out attempt. Yet at Göritten, it was the poor Russian command and control that limited their ability to respond to the German counter-attacks. The main lesson here is an obvious one – that the side with the better command and control was more likely to achieve its objectives – but what is less obvious is that the Germans made their share of mistakes, too.

German prisoners under guard by Russian infantry, apparently captured in autumn 1914. Both at Gumbinnen and Mahartse, the Russians took significant numbers of prisoners. Indeed, Russia took as many German prisoners on the Eastern Front as the Allies did on the Western Front in the opening year of the war. (From the fonds of the RGAKFD in Krasnogorsk via Stavka)

Aftermath

After Mahartse, the northern part of the Eastern Front settled down into static combat for months and the main action occurred further south in Poland. Both sides' pre-war infantry regiments had taken considerable losses in the first six months of combat on the Eastern Front, although a significant number of Russian regular units, like the bulk of the 27th Infantry Division, had been eliminated. The problem for the Russians was that their replacements and reserve divisions were not anywhere near the standard of their own pre-war regulars, so the drop in quality was noticeable by early 1915. On the opposing side, the German reserve units proved nearly as well-trained and effective as their regulars, so combat losses did not lead to a rapid deterioration in fighting ability.

A German dugout in East Prussia or Poland, complete with creature comforts. The sign marked 'Rummelsburg' refers to a location in East Berlin. The German infantrymen were not keen on winter campaigning and preferred to go into winter quarters as soon as practical. (Nik Cornish at www.stavka. org.uk)

Most accounts of the Eastern Front in 1914–15 tend to emphasize the German operational-level triumph at Tannenberg and the subsequent campaigning in Poland, which point towards a widening superiority of German troops over Russian troops. German accounts, embellished with wartime propaganda, depicted most of the early battles as major triumphs, when in fact the results tended to be more inconclusive. While it is true that the Germans had won some battles and inflicted about 650,000 casualties upon the Russian Army in the first six months, it is also true that the Russian infantry was still quite solid and capable of holding its ground and even inflicting occasional reverses. The German Army suffered about 250,000 casualties on the Eastern Front in 1914 and another 80,000 casualties in January–February 1915 – these victories were not cheap. In strategic terms, the Russian Army was actually winning against the Austro-Hungarian armies on the Galician Front and the Germans were increasingly obliged to divert divisions to bolster their flagging Austro-Hungarian allies. The outcome of the war in the Eastern Front was far from decided after the first six months and the Russian infantry remained a steadfast opponent.

Russian troops constructing field bunkers and deep bunkers in 1915 – the beginning of positional warfare on the Eastern Front. There was plenty of lumber available from local forests and the Russians proved quite adept at digging. (Courtesy of the Central Museum of the Armed Forces, Moscow via Stavka)

UNIT ORGANIZATIONS

At the beginning of World War I, the infantry corps was the basic unit of manoeuvre for most armies and each normally included two infantry divisions and an artillery brigade. Usually a cavalry unit was also attached to each infantry corps, although the size could vary from a squadron up to a brigade. Both the German and Russian Armies used 'square formations', which meant that infantry divisions were sub-divided into two infantry brigades, each controlling two infantry regiments. Below regimental level there was a bit more diversity, but all infantry battalions were comprised of four companies. The armies of 1914 were overwhelmingly comprised of infantry; in German infantry divisions, over 73 per cent of the personnel were infantrymen. Division support troops were kept an absolute minimum, which meant that logistical systems were rudimentary and closely tied to the nearest railhead. During General Mobilization, both the German and Russian regular infantry corps were brought up to full wartime strength by augmentation with reservists.

Russian

In August 1914, the Russian 3rd Corps (*3-i armeyskiy korpus*) was under the command of General-leytenant Nikolai A. Yepanchin and consisted of 25th and 27th Infantry divisions, 5th Rifle Brigade and 3rd Cavalry Division. Each infantry division was authorized a strength of 14,800 troops and consisted of two infantry brigades, each with two infantry regiments, and an artillery brigade. This meant that a full-strength Russian infantry corps at the start of the war had a total of 12 infantry regiments with 48,000 infantry and 108 artillery pieces (96 76.2mm guns and 12 122mm howitzers). In terms of infantry strength, the Russian corps had a considerable edge over the German infantry corps, but the German corps had a significant advantage in artillery over the Russian corps.

One of the regiments of General-leytenant August-Karl M. Adaridi's 27th Infantry Division, the 106th Infantry Regiment *Ufimsky*, had a nominal strength of about 4,000 troops and was led by Polkovnik Konstantin P. Otryganev. The *Ufimsky* Regiment consisted of four infantry battalions, an 84-man machine-gun detachment (*komanda*) equipped with 6–8 Maxim machine guns, a 64-man reconnaissance detachment and a 35-man communications detachment. Each Russian infantry regiment consisted of 16 companies, numbered sequentially. In wartime, an infantry company (*rota*) had an authorized combat strength of 224 troops (four officers, 40 NCOs and 180 privates) and was led by a *kapitan*. In the field, the Russian infantry company could either operate as four individual platoons (*vzvody*) of about 55 troops each or as two half-companies. Each infantry company was further sub-divided into 16 infantry squads, each squad (*otdeleniye*) led by a *yefreitor* or *mladshi unterofitser*.

German

Once mobilized, XVII. Armeekorps in Danzig started the war with eight infantry regiments (comprising 25 infantry battalions) with a total of about 27,000 infantrymen. XVII. Armeekorps also had 24 divisional field-artillery batteries (with 96 7.7cm guns and 36 10.5cm howitzers) and four corps-level heavy-artillery batteries (with 16 15cm howitzers), as well as eight cavalry squadrons, three pioneer companies and Feldflieger-Abteilung 17. The other two Stehendes Heer infantry corps in 8. Armee had similar strength and organization, but the Reserve and Landwehr formations had less artillery.

In 1914, a German first-line *Infanterie-Regiment* had an authorized strength of 3,287 troops and was led by an *Oberst*. The German regiment consisted of three infantry battalions and a machine-gun company with six MG 08s. The German regimental staff included a medical officer, a transport officer and 37 musicians for the band. Of note, each infantry regiment in 8. Armee had a numerical designation in the German Army as well as a separate regional designation.

After mobilization, a German *Infanterie-Bataillon* had up to 28 officers, 85 NCOs and over 960 enlisted men, for a nominal strength of around 1,080 men. It consisted of four infantry companies. The German infantry company had an authorized strength of 245 troops and was led by a *Hauptmann*. Each company was sub-divided into three 77-man platoons (*Züge*) and could be further sub-divided into a total of 12 sections (*Gruppen*).

A German infantry regiment marches out of its garrison with its musicians playing. This was great for boosting morale, but having 37 musicians in each infantry regiment was a significant diversion of manpower to an ancillary function. Although the Russian Army had some bands, they were not assigned down to regimental level. (Nik Cornish at www.stavka.org.uk)

BIBLIOGRAPHY

Belolipetsky, Valerian E. (1940). *Winter Activities Infantry Regiment in the August Woods, 1915*. Moscow: Military Publishing.

Buttar, Prit (2014). *Collision of Empires: The War on the Eastern Front in 1914*. Oxford: Osprey.

Cornish, Nik (2006). *The Russian Army and the First World War*. Stroud: Spellmount.

Estreyher-Egorov, R.A. (1936). *Boy oo Gyerrityen v avgoostye 1914 goda* ('Battle of Gerrit, August 1914'). Moscow: State Military Publishing.

Freytag-Lorin, Friedrich Philipp Johann (2009). *Das Exerzier-Reglement für die Infanterie Vom 29. Mai 1906 Kriegsgeschichtlich Erlautert* ('The Exercise Regulations for the Infantry from 29 May 1906'). Charleston, SC: BiblioBazaar.

Golovine, Nicholas M. (1933). *Russian Campaign of 1914: The Beginning of the War and Operations in East Prussia*. Leavenworth, KS: The Command and General Staff School Press.

Gurko, V. (1919). *War and Revolution in Russia 1914–1917*. New York, NY: Macmillan.

Izonov, V.V. (2004). 'Podgotovka russkoy armii nakanune Pervoy mirovoy voyny' ('Preparation of the Russian Army on the Eve of the First World War'), *Voyenno-istoricheskiy zhurnal* (*Military History Journal*) No. 10: 34–39.

Janz, Hermann D. (2013). *Die deutsche Ostfront 1914–1918: Der Kampf des deutschen Kaiserheeres im Osten und die Folgen* ('The German Eastern Front 1914-1918: The struggle of the German Imperial Army in the East and the consequences'). Munich: Grin Verlag GmbH.

Kharkevich, M. & Korsun, N.G. (1957). 'Taktika russkoi armii v pervuiu mirovuiu voinu 1914–1918 gg.' ('The tactics of the Russian Army in the World War of 1914–18') in *Razvitiye taktiki russkoy armii (XVIIIv.-nachalo XX v.): sbornik statey* ('Development of tactics of the Russian army (18th–beginning of 20th centuries): A collection of articles'). Moscow: USSR Ministry of Defence.

Knox, Sir Alfred (1921). *With the Russian Army, Being Chiefly Extracts from the Diary of a Military Attaché*, Volume 1. London: Hutchinson & Co.

Lasch, Wilhelm (1937). *Geschichte des 3. Unterelsässischen Infanterie-Regiments Nr. 138* ('History of the 3. Alsatian Infantry Regiment No. 138'). Saarbrücken: Verlag Saarbrücker Dr. u. Verl.

Lincoln, W. Bruce (1986). *Armageddon: The Russians in War and Revolution 1914–1918*. New York, NY: Simon & Schuster.

Mackensen, August von (1938). *Briefe und Auszeichnungen des Generalfeldmaschalls aus Krieg und Frieden* ('Awards and letters of Generalfeldmaschalls of war and peace'). Leipzig: Bibliographisches Institut.

Morgen, Curt von (1920). *Meiner Truppen Heldenkämpfe* ('My Heroic Fighting Troops'). Berlin: E.S. Mittler & Sohn.

Pahalyuk, Konstantin (2012). *The 27th Division in the Battles in East Prussia, 1914–15*. Kaliningrad: Reitar, Nr. 1 and Nr. 2.

Preusser, W. (1931). *Das 9. Westpreussisches Infanterie-Regiment Nr. 176 im Weltkrieg* ('The 9. West Prussian Infantry Regiment No. 176 in the World War'). Berlin: Verlag Tradition Kolk.

Showalter, Dennis E. (1991). *Tannenberg: Clash of Empires*. Hamden, CT: Archon Books.

Stone, Norman (1998). *The Eastern Front 1914–1917*. London: Penguin

Sweetman, John (2002). *Tannenberg 1914*. London: Cassell.

Tuchman, Barbara (2000). *The Guns of August*. London: Robinson.

Uspensky, A.A. (1932). *Na voynye. Vost. Proossiya – Litva* (*In the War, East Prussia – Lithuania*). Kaunas.

Zuber, Terence (2011). *The Real German War Plan 1904–14*. Stroud: The History Press.

A Russian infantry regiment on the march in August 1914, probably in Lithuania prior to crossing into East Prussia. Note the mounted officer at the front of the column. Like the Germans, the Russian infantry advanced in column but deployed into skirmish lines whenever contact occurred. (Author)

INDEX

Figures in **bold** refer to illustrations.